HASSOP
A CHRONOLOGY OF
RAILWAY HISTORY

by Laurence Knighton

FOREWORD

Hassop Station was situated 153 miles 65 chains from St Pancras on the Derby to Manchester main line between Bakewell and Great Longstone[1] stations. It was the station for Baslow and one of the three stations for Chatsworth, the home of the Duke of Devonshire, the others being Rowsley and Bakewell. The Hassop Station Inn, which was situated adjacent to the station entrance was constructed by the Chatsworth Estate. Probably because of these factors, the passenger station was one of the large and imposing structures on the line rather than the cottage type to be seen at neighbouring Great Longstone Station.

It was always 'a busy place' as far as goods traffic was concerned, with spar and stone traffic forwarded and coal traffic received. Cattle and cattle cake were important traffics as well as grain and raw cotton / yarn associated with Calver Mill.

Hardly a dwelling could be seen from the station, Hassop itself being a hamlet rather than a village, with the result that passenger traffic was not buoyant and the rather minimal service of trains was withdrawn from 17th August 1942.

Examination of the official *Traffic and Expenses at Stations* statistics shows that 8,913 passengers were booked in 1872 (compared with 6,276 at Longstone and 16,451 at Millers Dale) and 9,686 in 1875, but then there was a steady decline from the middle 1890s reaching abysmal figures of 2,099 in 1915, 2,766 in 1920 and 1,760 in 1922. On the other hand, bookings at Millers Dale more that doubled between 1872 and 1922. This would indicate abstraction of passengers by other stations. Once semi-fast or express trains began calling at Bakewell, that station would have become more attractive to the traveller than its neighbour, at which some stopping trains now ceased to call.

Who travelled from Hassop station in the days of enterprising 'bus services and the motor car? The service was quite frankly poor from 1931, perhaps best summed up by Alan Casey[2] whilst at Bakewell just before the war '... *once collected 1½ d excess from a passenger who had started his journey from Hassop to Manchester and the return train did not stop*'

Once a Derby to Manchester line had been projected and opened, there were many schemes for a branch from that route in the vicinity of Hassop towards Sheffield, one of the objectives being to connect Sheffield and Buxton.

These schemes can be summarised as:

1844 / 6	North Derbyshire Union Railway. (Ashford & Dronfield)
1845	Sheffield, Bakewell & West Midland Railway
1863	Sheffield, Chesterfield & Staffordshire Railway
1871	M R (Hassop & Dore) line
1885	Hassop & Padley Railway
1903	Grindleford, Baslow & Bakewell Railway
1920	Derwent Valley, Calver & Bakewell Railway

Part of the objective was achieved with the opening of the Dore & Chinley route more than a hundred years ago. However, the fact that a line was not constructed from Hassop to Grindleford is more surprising than if it had been built.

Operationally, Hassop provided a useful function. The signalbox was open continuously whilst Bakewell was switched out on the night shift, thus the Down lie bye was available for the recessing of freight trains throughout the day. Also run round / recessing facilities were available for coaching stock at holiday times and on Sundays.

Hassop served the community well and these notes are dedicated to the staff who worked there over the years.

Laurence Knighton

---

[1] Opened as Longstone on 1st June 1863 and renamed Great Longstone for Ashford on 1st October 1913.
[2] Alan Casey commenced his railway career at Rowsley. He subsequently became a Booking Clerk at Bakewell, a controller at Rowsley and the District Inspector at Rowsley. He retired as the Assistant Area Manager (Operating) at Toton.

ACKNOWLEDGEMENTS

I am grateful to the following former railway colleagues and friends for providing information about Hassop station:

Herbert Bond	Les Harrison	Ken Munns
Alan Casey	Mrs Hart (widow of Jack)	David Nutall
Tom Chapman	Philip Horne	Ken Robinson
Hilary Clarke	Arthur Miles	Jesse Rosling
Harry Dearing	Mrs M. Moseley	Bill Wild
Lawrence Gratton	J. Mullins (son of Tom)	

I am also indebted to Mary Adlen for typing the manuscript and to Glynn Waite and Nick Wheat for the production of this book.

Unless otherwise shown, photographs and illustrations in this publication are from the author's collection.

The following Midland Railway Society publication may also be of interest to readers:

Rowsley : A Rural Railway Centre, by Glynn Waite and Laurence Knighton. 128pages, with over 250 illustrations, many not previously published. Available in hardback at £19.95 and softback at £15.95.

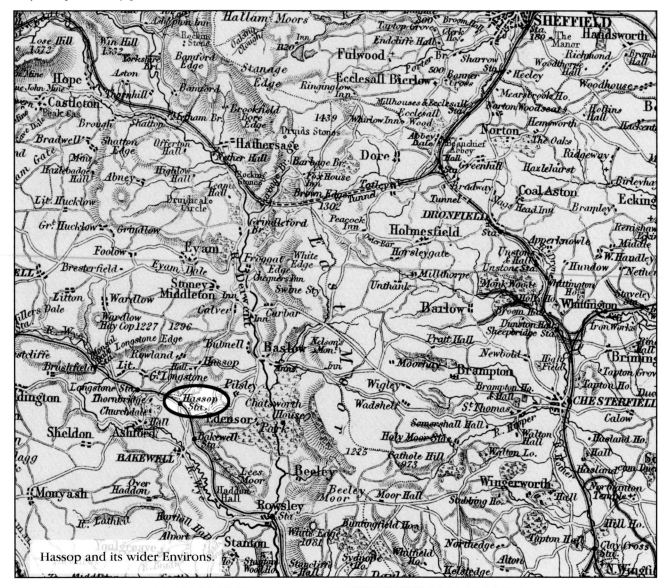

Hassop and its wider Environs.

THE CHRONOLOGY

There were many entries between 1860 and 1863 in the Midland Railway (Rowsley & Buxton) Construction Committee Minute Book now held at the Public Record Office at Kew. Many of the entries for that period have come from this source.

6th June 1860	W.H. Barlow appointed Engineer for the Midland Railway's Rowsley & Buxton line.
1st August 1860	Plans, Sections and Specifications completed. Centre line is staked out throughout the whole of the first contract.
13th August 1860	George Thomson & Co's tender of £39,198.0s.0d for Contract No1 (Rowsley and Longstone) accepted.
March 1861	1,391 men and 91 horses employed on the two contracts from Rowsley to Longstone and Longstone to Buxton.
August 1861	1,979 men and 142 horses now employed. In the meanwhile, a community of construction workers at Harrison Lane is revealed in the 1861 Census. These consisted of:

August 1861: Rail Road Driver, Carter (2), Excavator, Railway Tip Driver (2), Railway Construction (3) and Railway Carter.

Harrison Lane, which ran between Baslow Road and Hassop Road was 'stopped' as a result of the building of the line. This lane was an extension of Gypsy Lane towards the site that became Hassop station. Work was taking place near to Pineapple Farm at that time – the Pineapple Inn offering useful facilities to the contractor's workmen.

2nd October 1861	The Engineer suggested that the line should be signalled by Telegraphs.
4th February 1862	Mr Kirtley, the Locomotive Superintendent was *'to test water for locomotives'*, while *'Sir Joseph Paxton be requested to arrange terms for the supply of water to a reservoir from springs on the Duke of Devonshire's land for locomotive and station purposes'*.

Water Supply – Gravitation from Springs

The water supply was taken from the wood / springs above the Pineapple to Birchills Lodge Road. There was a 16" stone drain to a catch pit (where there was a connection to cottages, now Birchill House), a 4" pipe to a reservoir at the corner of the field near Flat Plantation off Baslow Road, thence an 8" main to the station. A farm (trough) near the station was supplied through a ¾" pipe. A payment of £3 per annum was paid to the Duke of Devonshire. The Midland Railway was entitled to take water for all purposes provided that cottages and certain troughs had first call.

4th February 1862 — The tender of John Wood for the construction of the stations at Rowsley, Bakewell and Hassop was accepted. This consisted of:

Stations and platforms	£6,455. 7s.6d
Iron roof columns, etc. to shed over platform	£2,109.15s.0d
	£8,565. 2s.6d

The average cost of each station was about £2,855.

The construction was to be completed by 10th June 1862. A penalty of £10 per day was to be levied if the work was not completed by that date.

7th May 1862	Contract for the construction of the Water Station let to George Scothorne of Matlock.
1st August 1862	Hassop station opened to passenger traffic – the temporary terminus of the branch from Ambergate.

Details of the initial train service are summarised on page 4. The staff appointed with the opening of the station were:-
Station Master
Clerk
Signal Porter
Porter
Assistant Porter (appointment subsequently dispensed with)
Office Cleaner

THE INITIAL TRAIN SERVICE TO AND FROM HASSOP

The following summarises the weekday service. Unless shown otherwise, all trains called at Whatstandwell Bridge, Cromford, Matlock Bath, Matlock Bridge, Darley, Rowsley and Bakewell.

	A			A	A	A	A B
	am	am	am	pm	pm	pm	pm
Ambergate	6.40	9.25	11.30	2.25	3.55	7.00	9.25
Hassop	7.30	10.10	12.20	3.15	4.45	7.50	10.10

A = Through train from Derby, with reversal and 10 minutes stop at Ambergate.
B = Did not call at Darley.

	C		C	C	D	C
	am	am	pm	pm	pm	pm
Hassop	8.00	10.20	12.45	4.30	6.50	8.15
Ambergate	8.50	11.00	1.35	5.20	7.37	9.05

C = Through train to Derby, with reversal and 10 minutes stop at Ambergate.
D = Through train to Derby, with reversal and 8 minutes stop at Ambergate.

It is not explained what happened to the engine and coaches off the 9/25 from Ambergate to Hassop. It is possible that the engine went on to Rowsley shed for the night and that both engine and coaches went forward to Ambergate attached the 8.00 departure from Hassop on the following day, where they were detached for the 9.25 return service.

There was one 'all stations' train each way on Sundays. The Down train left Derby at 10.00, reversed at Ambergate (10.30-10.40) and arrived at Hassop at 11.30. It returned from Hassop at 5/45, reversed at Ambergate (6/35-6/45) and arrived at Derby at 7/15.

It will be noted that the timetable was designed to be worked (mainly) from the Derby / Ambergate end – probably as a prelude to through working to Buxton. However, by January 1863 (see page 5), the service had been altered substantially to show two trains starting from Hassop before the arrival of an inwards service from Ambergate.

Front

Back

Robert Thornhill was an active member of the community at Longstone, also being Clerk to the Commissioners of Taxes, and High Constable for the High Peak Hundred. His journeys increased with the expanding rail network. Fortunately his diary for 1862 survives, with interesting entries.

On 9th July he *'went to London from Rowsley, first class fare 14/-'*. He returned on 12th July leaving *'London at 2.30pm and arriving home after 11.0pm'*. The entry for 1st August, when Hassop station opened, reads *'At noon to Bakewell by train from Hassop'*. Noon would have been the time he left his home to catch the 12.45pm train from Hassop.

The reason why half of the ticket (left) was kept for many years was to be found in a note written to Ann, who was either his wife or daughter. Robert tells her that he had taken *'her letter to Bakewell to post and had forgotten it'*, and also *'that we have just got in from Bakewell at 4.15pm'*. He also commented that it was *'almost as far from Bakewell Station to the Town as from here (Longstone) to Hassop Station'*, and that there *'were 4 of us first class there and back and as proof I enclose a ticket'*.

On 8th October of the same year he *'sent a hamper by train to Kings Cross from Hassop, paid 2s.7d'*, and a fortnight later travelled to London with a first class return that cost him 14/-. Early in the following year a hamper with a haunch of venison was sent to London.

6th August 1862	John Wood's tender of £275 for the construction of the Station House accepted. To be of stone.
1st September 1862	Question of flagging the station platform to be postponed until spring.
29th September 1862	John Wood's tender of £500 for the construction of the Goods Shed accepted. Also included the crane.
29th September 1862	Report of Progress of Works states *'As arranged, the line is prepared to receive mineral traffic from 1st October'*.
	It was also reported that *'The Permanent Way and Ballasting is now in progress beyond Hassop, a length of about one mile single having been laid'*.
1st November 1862	Hassop Station opened for goods traffic.

December 1862 — Signal and Telegraph communication between Hassop and Buxton: Contract for the erection of signals given to William Abell of Derby, who had previously supplied semaphore signals at £24.10s.0d each and Distant Signals at £18.5s.0d each. The telegraph was put in the hands of Mr Warwick, Electric & International Telephone Co.[3]

Miles from Ambergate	DOWN	WEEK DAYS. 1w	2w	3w	4w	5w				SUNDS 1w	2	FARES from DERBY.		
	TRAINS LEAVE	a.m.	a.m.	a.m.	p.m.	p.m				a.m.				
	LONDON King's Cross ..	..		11 30	..	5 35	..	..	..	..	..	..	..	..
	LONDON (Euston Station)	..	6 15	11 0	..	5 0	..	..	..		..	..	..	..
	BIRMINGHAM	..	8 45	..	3 50	6 50	..	..	..	7 15	..	..	..	..
	NOTTINGHAM	8 5	9 35	2 35	3 45	8 0	..	..	..	9 0	..	..	..	..
	DERBY	9 25	10 15	3 30	6 20	8 35	..	..	..	10 0	..	..	..	..
	Duffield	9 35	..	3 40	6 30	..	..	..	..	10 15	..	..	..	..
	Belper	9 40	10 41	3 45	6 35	9 3	..	..	..	10 21	..	..	..	..
	LEEDS	6 0	8 20	1 0	..	4 55	..	..	..	7 0	..	..	..	..
	NORMANTON..........	6 33	8 50	1 33	..	5 35	..	..	..	7 30	..	..	..	..
	SHEFFIELD	7 25	9 35	2 10	..	6 30	..	..		8 15	..	..	..	..
	Ambergate, arr. fr. South	9 50	10 51	3 55	6 45	9 10	..	..	..	10 30	..	..	..	..
	Ambergate, arr. fr. North	9 20	11 22	3 51	..	8 28	..	..	..	10 15	..	..	..	..
		1 2 gov. a.m.	1 2 class a.m.	1 2 class p.m.	1 2 gov p.m.	1 2 class p.m.				gov. 1 2 class a.m		1st clas s. d.	2nd clas s. d.	gov s. d.
	AMBERGATE ......dep.	10 0	11 30	4 5	6 50	9 15	..	..	..	10 40	..	..		..
2¼	Whatstandwell Bridge ..	10 7	11 37	4 12	6 55	9 21	..	..	..	10 47	..	2 3	1 8	1 0½
5	Cromford	10 15	11 45	4 20	7 2	9 28	..	..	..	10 55	..	2 5	1 9	1 3
6	MATLOCK-BATH	10 18	11 48	4 23	7 5	9 31	..	..	..	10 58	..	2 6	1 10	1 4
7	Matlock Bridge	10 21	11 51	4 26	7 8	9 34	..	..	..	11 1	..	2 9	2 0	1 5
9¼	Darley	10 27	11 56	4 32	7 13	.	..	..	..	11 6	..	3 3	2 3	1 7
11½	ROWSLEY	10 35	12 5	4 40	7 20	9 45	..	..	..	11 15	..	3 6	2 6	1 9
15	BAKEWELL	10 45	12 15	4 50	7 30	9 55	..	..	..	11 25	..	4 4	3 2	2 0½
16	HASSOP	10 50	12 20	4 55	7 35	10 0	.	..	..	11 30	..	4 6	3 3	2 1½
..	BUXTON (by Coach) arr.	12 45	2 15	6 50	..	..	..	..	..	..	..	8 6	5 "	..

HASSOP, ROWSLEY, and MATLOCK-BATH to AMBERGATE.—UP.

Miles from Hassop	The Classes of Trains shewn in this Table refer only to Stations between Rowsley & Ambergate.	WEEK DAYS. 1w	2w	3w	4w	5w				SUNDS. 1w	2	FARES from HASSOP. 1st clas	2nd clas	gov clas
		1 2 class gov.	1 2 class	1 2 class	1 2 class	1 2 class				1 2 class gov.				
	TRAINS LEAVE	a.m.	a.m.	noon	p.m.	p m.				p.m.		s. d.	s. d	s. d.
..	BUXTON (by Coach)	..	..	10 40	2 25	4 0	..	..	..		..	..	..	
..	HASSOP	7 45	10 0	1 0	4 30	7 45	..	..	..	5 45	..	..	..	
1	BAKEWELL	7 50	10 5	1 5	4 35	7 48	..	..	..	5 50	..	0 4	0 2	One Penny per Mile
4½	ROWSLEY	8 0	10 15	1 15	4 45	7 57	..	..	..	6 0	..	1 0	0 9	
6¾	Darley	8 7	10 21	1 21	4 52	..	..	..	..	6 6	..	1 4	1 0	
9	Matlock Bridge	8 12	10 27	1 27	4 58	8 6	..	..	..	6 13	..	1 10	1 4	
10	MATLOCK-BATH	8 15	10 31	1 31	5 1	8 9	..	..	..	6 16	..	2 0	1 6	
11	Cromford	8 18	10 35	1 35	5 4	8 12	..	..	..	6 20	..	2 2	1 8	
13¾	Whatstandwell Bridge ..	8 27	10 41	1 42	5 12	..	..	..	..	6 27	..	2 8	2 0	
16	AMBERGATE ......arr.	8 35	10 48	1 50	5 20	8 25	..	..	..	6 35	..	3 2	2 2	
..	Ambergate dep. for North	..	10 51	1 53	5 26	.	..	..	..	6 43	..	..	..	..
..	Ambergate dep. for South	8 45	11 22	2 0	5 25	8 28	..	..	..	6 45	..			.
..	SHEFFIELD	..	12 35	3 40	7 15	10 15	..	..	..	8 20	..	9 2	6 8	..
..	NORMANTON	..	1 3	4 23	8 10	10 30	..	..	.	9 15	..	12 10	9 10	..
..	LEEDS		1 30	5 5	8 45	11 0	..	..	..	9 45	..	14 10	11 6	..
..	Belper	8 54	11 30	2 9	5 34	8 36	..	..	..	6 52	..	3 9	2 9	1 7
..	Duffield	9 0	..	2 15	5 40	8 43	..	..	..	6 58	..	4 0	3 0	1 9
..	DERBY..............	9 15	11 50	2 30	5 55	9 0	..	..	..	7 15	..	4 6	3 3	2 1½
..	NOTTINGHAM	10 50	12 55	3 35	7 10	10 10	..	..	..	8 10	..	6 6	4 8	..
..	BIRMINGHAM	12 15	1 45	4 45	9 25	2 2	..	..	..	9 30	..	12 0	8 9	5 7½
..	LONDON, Euston Station	3 45	5 15	7 0	11 16	5 50	..	..	..	6 0	..	30 3	22 6	12 8
..	LONDON, King's Cross..	3 40	3 40	6 10	10 5	..	..	..	..	...	..	30 3	22 6	12 8

By January 1863, the weekday service between Derby, Ambergate and Hassop had been reduced to five trains in each direction and appears to have been worked entirely from the Hassop end – although it is not clear from this public timetable extract whether any of the services ran to / from Derby to change rolling stock and men. There were now two departures from Hassop before the first arrival from Ambergate and two sets of coaches appear to have been stabled there at night (with the engines going light to and from Rowsley shed). The Sunday services remained unaltered and continued to be worked from the Derby end.

The timetable, which had the impressive heading *'MATLOCK, BAKEWELL, CHATSWORTH, BUXTON &c. – AMBERGATE TO MATLOCK-BATH, ROWSLEY, and HASSOP'* had a number of notes down the side, which it has not been possible to copy, due to the spine of the book. There was information relating to a conveyance between Cromford and Wirksworth and an omnibus between Rowsley and Chatsworth. Of relevance to Hassop was *'An Omnibus meets all the Trains at the Bakewell station and Post Horses may be had at either the Rowsley, Bakewell, or Hassop Stations'*. A further note stated that *'Passengers booked through to and from Buxton are conveyed by the Coach to and from Bakewell instead of Rowsley, as heretofore'*. So while the trains started from and terminated at Hassop, this was not where the Buxton connections were made.

The single fare of 4d First Class and 2d Second Class for the one mile journey between Hassop and Bakewell would certainly have deterred the ordinary workman from making such a journey. There was, of course, the statutory 1d a mile Government Class accommodation, which was introduced in 1844 to prevent exploitation of passengers. However, railways were obliged to convey such carriages on only one train per day in each direction. It will be noted that there were two weekday services from Ambergate with such carriages, but only one from Hassop. It is assumed that all the Government Class carriages were conveyed on the 7.45am train from Hassop, but were spilt at Ambergate so that they could return on the two services shown.

1st March 1863 — The index to the Midland Railway timetable shows Hassop as the nearest station for Ashford and Baslow, both 2½ miles distant. Hitherto, Rowsley was shown as the nearest station to Ashford (5 miles) and Chesterfield for Baslow (8 miles)!

Hassop was also shown as the nearest station for Great Longstone (2miles) and Little Longstone (2½ miles), and had been since at least January 1863.

1st April 1863 — Mr Allport, the General Manager of the Midland Railway, to arrange for the procurement and fixing of the necessary Goods and Yard Cranes where required at stations.

2nd April 1863 — Agreed that *'such portions of the platform as are under the glass roofs be formed of timber and the remaining parts outside asphalted'*.

6th May 1863 — John Woods's tender of £150 for alterations to platforms accepted, subject to satisfying the Engineer as to the terms upon which he will burnetize the timbers.

1st June 1863 — Line opened from Hassop to Buxton, with intermediate stations at Longstone and Millers Dale.

8th June 1863 — Recorded that Mr Wood's tender for the completion of the platforms had been accepted.

1st July 1863 — Line from Hassop to Buxton opened for goods traffic.

[3] J.A. Warwick was later the Telegraph Superintendent of the Midland Railway.

76 BUXTON AND MATLOCK BRANCH.

Table 25. AMBERGATE and MATLOCK to BUXTON.

Miles from Derby	DOWN	WEEK DAYS. 1w	2w	3w	4w	5w	6w	7w		SUNDS. 1w	2	FARES from DERBY.		
	TRAINS LEAVE	a.m.	a.m.	a.m.	a.m.	a.m	p.m.	p.m.		a.m.	p.m.			
	LONDON King's Cross ..	..	..	..	9 20	11 30	..	5 35	..	..	..	..	..	..
	LONDON (Euston Station)	..	..	6 15	9 0	11 0	..	5 0	..	..	..	..	..	..
	BIRMINGHAM	..	..	8 45	11 30		3 25	6 50	..	..	..	..	..	..
	NOTTINGHAM	6 25	8 10	9 40	12 35	2 30	5 40	8 10	..	7 15	6 50	..	..	..
	LEEDS	..	6 0	8 20	..	1 0	..	4 55	..	..	3 0	..	..	..
	NORMANTON..........	..	6 33	8 50	..	1 33	..	5 35	..	..	3 35	..	..	..
	SHEFFIELD	..	7 25	9 35	..	2 10	..	6 30	..	..	4 15	..	..	..
		1 2 gov.	1 2 class	1 2 class	1 2 class	1 2 class	1 2 gov	1 2 class		1 2 gov.	1 2 gov.	1st clas	2nd clas	gov
		a.m.	a.m.	a.m.	p.m	p.m.	p.m.	p. m.		a.m	p. m.	s. d.	s. d.	s. d.
..	DERBY	7 20	9 0	10 35	1 45	3 30	6 40	8 55	..	8 0	7 30	..	..	..
5½	Duffield	7 30	9 10	..	..	3 40	6 50	..	..	8 10	7 40	1 2	0 10	0 5½
7¼	Belper	7 35	9 15	10 51	..	3 45	6 55	9 8		8 15	7 45	1 6	1 0	0 7
10¼	AMBERGATE J. arr.	7 43	9 23	11 0	2 3	3 51	7 3	9 14		8 23	7 53	2 0	1 6	0 10
	AMBERGATE J. dep.	7 47	9 27	11 30	2 7	3 55	7 7	9 18	..	8 27	7 57			
12¾	Whatstandwell Bridge ..	7 54	9 34	..	2 13	..	7 14	..	..	8 34	8 4	2 3	1 8	1 0½
15¼	Cromford	8 2	9 42	11 42	2 20	4 7	7 22	9 30	..	8 42	8 12	2 5	1 9	1 3
16¼	MATLOCK-BATH	8 5	9 45	11 45	2 23	4 10	7 25	9 33	..	8 45	8 15	2 6	1 10	1 4
17¼	Matlock Bridge	8 8	9 48	11 48	2 26	4 13	7 28	9 36	..	8 48	8 18	2 9	2 0	1 5
19½	Darley	8 13	9 53	..	2 31	..	7 33	..	..	8 53	8 23	3 3	2 3	1 7
21¾	Rowsley.................	8 20	10 0	11 58		4 23	7 40	9 46	..	9 0	8 30	3 6	2 6	1 9
25	BAKEWELL	8 31	10 11	12 7	2 43	4 32	7 51	9 55	..	9 11	8 41	4 4	3 2	2 0½
26	Hassop	8 35	10 15	..	2 46	4 35	7 55	9 58	..	9 15	8 45	4 6	3 3	2 1½
27¼	Longstone	8 40	10 20	[illegible]	2 51		8 0	..	..	9 20	8 50	5 0	3 4	2 2½
31½	Miller's Dale	8 50	10 30	12 21		4 46	8 10	10 19	..	9 30	9 0	5 10	4 0	2 6½
37	BUXTON .... arr.	9 10	10 50	12 40	3 20	5 5	8 30	10 30	..	9 50	9 20	6 9	4 9	3 0

BUXTON and MATLOCK to AMBERGATE.—UP.

Miles from Buxton	The Classes of Trains shewn in this Table refer only to Stations between Buxton & Derby.	WEEK DAYS. 1w	2w	3w	4w	5w	6w	7w		SUNDS. 1w	2	FARES from BUXTON.		
		1 2 gov.	1 2 class	1 2 class	1 2 class	1 2 class	1 2 class	1 2 gov.		1 2 gov.	1 2 gov.	1st clas	2nd clas	gov clas
	TRAINS LEAVE	a.m.	a m	a.m.	p.m.	p m.	p m.	p.m.		a.m.	p.m.	s. d.	s. d	s. d.
..	BUXTON	6 30	9 35	10 15	12 45	2 15	4 45	7 0	..	8 0	7 30	..		
5½	Miller's Dale..........	6 48	9 51	10 32	..	2 32	5 1	7 17	..	8 17	7 47	1 2	0 10	0 5½
9½	Longstone	6 57	..	10 42	..	2 41	..	7 26	..	8 26	7 56	2 0	1 6	0 9½
11	Hassop	7 2	..	10 48	1 9	2 46	5 13	7 31	..	8 31	8 1	2 4	1 10	0 11
12	BAKEWELL	7 6	10 4	10 52	1 12	2 50	5 17	7 35	..	8 35	8 5	2 8	2 0	1 0
15¼	Rowsley...............	7 15	10 12	11 1	..	2 59	5 25	7 44	..	8 44	8 14	3 4	2 4	1 3
17½	Darley	7 21	..	..	1 23	3 4	..	7 49	..	8 49	8 19	3 8	2 6	1 5½
19¾	Matlock Bridge	7 26	10 23	11 11	1 28	3 9	5 35	7 54	..	8 54	8 24	4 2	2 10	1 7½
20¼	MATLOCK-BATH	7 29	10 26	11 15	1 31	3 12	5 38	7 57	..	8 57	8 27	4 4	3 0	1 8½
21½	Cromford	7 32	10 29	11 18	1 34	3 15	5 41	8 0	..	9 0	8 30	4 6	3 2	1 9½
24¼	Whatstandwell Bridge ..	7 38	..	..	..	3 21	..	8 7	..	9 7	8 37	5 0	3 8	2 0
26¼	AMBERGATE J. arr.	7 44	10 40	11 30	1 45	3 26	5 54	8 13	..	9 15	8 45	5 6	4 0	2 2½
	AMBERGATE J. dep.	7 48	11 22	11 34	1 49	3 30	5 58	8 17	..	9 19	8 49			
29¾	Belper	7 55	11 30	11 42	1 58	3 39	6 5	8 25	.	9 26	8 57	6 0	4 4	2 5½
31½	Duffield	8 0		..	2 4	3 45	6 10	..	..	9 30	9 3	6 4	4 6	2 7
37	DERBY...............	8 15	11 50	12 0	2 20	4 0	6 25	8 45	..	9 45	9 15	6 9	4 9	3 0
..	SHEFFIELD	..	11 55		3 40	..	8 30	..	..	..	..	8 0	6 0	..
..	NORMANTON	..	12 8	..	4 22	..	9 15	.	..	..	..	10 0	7 0	..
..	LEEDS	..	12 30	..	5 5		9 55		..	..	..	10 0	7 0	..
..	NOTTINGHAM	9 50		12 55	3 20	5 25	7 15	10 10	..	10 25	9 55	3 9	6 3	..
..	BIRMINGHAM	12 15	..	1 45	5 5	6 45	9 3[illegible]	..	..	..	..	10 0	7 6	6 6
..	LONDON, Euston Station	2 30	..		7 5	9 15	11 10	..	..	..	..	..	..	..
..	LONDON, King's Cross..	1 40	..	3 40	6 10	..	10 5	..	..	..	..	32 0	24 0	13 6½

The inaugural timetable of 1st June 1863 showing the service between Derby and Buxton. Also opened on this day was the new south curve at Ambergate, which allowed through running between Derby and Buxton without a reversal, while Ambergate station was re-sited at the point where the Leeds and Buxton lines diverged. It will be noted that 6 of the 7 weekday trains called at Hassop, while there were now two trains in each direction on Sundays. The note about Post Horses being available at Hassop station was still included, but there was now a new note, which read *'HASSOP – Omnibuses for Chatsworth meet all Trains at the Hassop Station, except the 6.30am from Buxton and the 7.20am from Derby'*. The entry about connections at Rowsley for Chatsworth now read *'ROWSLEY – Omnibuses to & from Chatsworth meet Nos.2, 3 & 5 Up and Down Trains at the Rowsley Station'*. So Hassop had now become the more important station for Chatsworth.

July 1863

Two Architects plans on fragile tracings, which were prepared during this month, survive locally, and show what was originally planned. [note that this is 11 months **after** the opening of the station!]

They are by Edward Walters (1808-1872), the Manchester Architect, who was best known for the Free Trade Hall and several of that city's warehouses. He designed the Midland stations at Chapel-en-le-Frith, Hassop, Bakewell and Rowsley, and did work on the London Extension from Bedford.

The plans are:

No.1 – Block Plan drawn to a scale of 16 feet to 1 inch showing drains etc. Veranda roof water was to be carried away through the platform columns. Urinal on Down platform.

No.11 – Ground Plan drawn to a scale of 6 feet to 1 inch. There are certain differences from the station as known:

a) Telegraph Office where Station Master's office existed.
b) Booking Hall 29'.9" x 21'.0" – i.e. Booking Hall and Booking Office combined – without central partition, but with the two fireplaces. A small Booking Office was partitioned within the Booking Hall opposite the entrance porch.

[It is clear the subsequent partition between the Booking Hall and Booking Office was an architectural afterthought, possibly during the first years or so of the station,]

c) 2nd and 3rd Class Waiting Room where 3rd Class Gents Waiting Room situated.

December 1863	A payment of £74.17s.0d made to John Wood for telegraph boxes and fittings at Hassop, Millers Dale and Buxton.
1863	Proposed Sheffield, Chesterfield & Staffordshire Railway, connecting with the Midland Railway at Hassop but proceeding over Lumford near Bakewell on arches. This was a rival scheme to the Midland's direct Chesterfield to Sheffield New Line, which was eventually constructed, and opened on 1st February 1870.
January 1864	A payment of £28.0s.0d made to John Wood for point boxes at Hassop, Millers Dale and Buxton and alterations to a bridge at Buxton.
1864	Abraham Wheeldon is recorded as the licensee of Hassop Station Inn (see foreword).
1864	Included in *Black's Tourist's Guide to Derbyshire* is an advert for Jepson's Chatsworth Hotel, Edensor, which states that an omnibus for Chatsworth meets every train at Hassop and that cabs and post horses were also available at the station. In later years, the Chatsworth Hotel omnibus met trains at Rowsley.

DERBYSHIRE.

JEPSON'S CHATSWORTH HOTEL

THE PUBLIC are respectfully informed that, through the extension of the Midland Railway from HASSOP, *via* Buxton for Manchester, etc., a greater facility is offered to parties wishing to visit

CHATSWORTH, HADDON HALL

and all the romantic scenery of the Peak. The Proprietor of the Chatsworth Hotel desires to inform the public, that Hassop is the station for Chatsworth, Haddon, etc., where cabs and post horses are always in readiness. An omnibus meets every train at Hassop for Chatsworth ; fare, 6d.

N.B.—Gentlemen staying at the Chatsworth Hotel can be supplied with tickets for fly-fishing in the river Derwent.

A Coffee Room for Ladies.

The advertisement for Jepson's Chatsworth Hotel in the 1864 edition of *Black's Tourist's Guide to Derbyshire*.

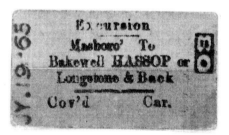

An excursion ticket from Masboro' (Rotherham) to Bakewell, Hassop and Longstone issued on 19th July 1865. The fact that Hassop is in capital letters indicates that this was the main destination and that most passengers would be bound for Chatsworth. *'Cov'd Car.'* would have been an abbreviation for Covered Carriage. Although all regular services conveyed such vehicles – this was a stipulation of the 1844 Act along with the 1d a mile fares – there was no requirement to provide covered carriages on excursion trains, where the fares charged could be less than 1d per mile. Note that the Midland Railway did not show its title on tickets at this time.

[G. Waite collection]

CHATSWORTH.—Omnibuses to and from Rowsley meet all the Trains, except the 6.25 a.m. & 12.40 p.m. from Buxton, & 7.30 a.m from Derby.
HASSOP.—Post-Horses and Flys are always in readiness on the arrival of the Trains appointed to stop at this Station.
A Coach meets the 9.15 a.m. Train from Buxton for Haddon Hall & Chatsworth, returning in time for the 4.50 or 7.23 p.m. Trains to Buxton.

An extract from the *'Matlock & Buxton Branch'* timetable for August 1865. Note that while Post Horses and Flys meet every train at Hassop and that there is a coach connection with specified trains to and from Buxton, the Omnibus connections are entirely with Rowsley. Six trains still call at Hassop in the Up direction but only four now call in the Down.

1865	Coal offices erected. These were similar in style to those at Bakewell, Millers Dale and Buxton. The contractor was probably the same, William Ward.
1866	Rail Weigh Office and Machine erected. This was a stone built structure, the contractor being C. Palmer.

1866	In the four years since the station opened, staff had been transferred to Hassop from:

Asfordby	Codnor Park	Manton
Bedford	Desborough	Matlock Bath
Berkley Road	Ilkeston	Wooden Box[4]
Charfield	Kettering	

This indicates that experienced staff were required for the opening of new lines and stations. The individual from Charfield resigned, which may suggest he was homesick for the warmth of rural Gloucestershire.

In the same period staff were promoted to:-

Ambergate	Birmingham	Sheffield
Bakewell	Leeds	Trent
Bedford		

Two clerks had the same surname as the Station Master – which was Buxton. Their salaries were low, suggesting youth. They were possibly the Station Master's sons.

Midland Railway Second Class tickets are extremely rare, as the company withdrew such facilities on 1st January 1875 – on which date Government Class became Third Class. This ticket would have been printed for the opening of the line in June 1863 and indicates that around 100 single tickets would have been issued each year for Second Class journeys between Millers Dale and Hassop. Tickets at this time were coloured according to the direction of travel. This one is blue. A ticket for a journey in the opposite direction would have been pink.   [G. Waite collection]

March 1870	At some date after March 1870, but before May 1871, Bradshaw[5] started to refer to the station as *'Hassop for Chatsworth'*. This continued until c.1906.
30th April 1870	*'Dog run over by express train*
	On Tuesday Mr Buxton of Hassop Station lost a favourite dog by the express train cutting it in two. Cats often come to that untimely end but dogs are generally more cautious.'
	From the *High Peak News*
October 1870	Prospectus issued for the Hassop, Hathersage & Castleton Railway. This was a purely local scheme – a single line of some 13 miles – which avoided the expense of a through route. The cost was to be £57.000, including land.
November 1871	Proposed Midland Railway (Hassop & Dore) line.

The first real scheme to specifically join Hassop with the Midland Railway near Sheffield.

What the papers said:

'The announcement that the Midland Company are preparing to deposit plans for a line from Abbeydale to Hassop, cannot fail to give general satisfaction.'
                                        Derby Mercury

'The line will be enormously expensive for the length, as it will probably involve some four miles of tunnel.'   *Sheffield Independent*

The scheme was not proceeded with.

Late 1874	Down lie bye provided for the regulation of trains.
11th October 1876	The license of Hassop Station Inn is granted to Ann Wheeldon, presumably on the death of her husband.

This type of glass slotted into the lamp cases on the platform lamps in an attempt to assist station identification. It was perhaps removed when war broke out!

---

[4] Later known as Woodville.
[5] The publisher of monthly 'all company' railway timetables.

TIDESWELL.—The Tideswell Coach meets the following Trains at the Miller's Dale Station :—8.0 a.m. and 3.40 p.m., Derby to Buxton and Manchester, and 7.55 a.m. and 3.35 p.m. Manchester to Derby.
HASSOP.—An Omnibus for Chatsworth meets the 7.55 and 11.35 a.m. Trains from Manchester, returning from Chatsworth in time to meet the 4.54 p.m. Train, Hassop to Buxton and Manchester.
BAKEWELL.—Omnibuses from the Rutland Arms Hotel meet all Trains, and Post Horses from there may be had at the Bakewell Station.
ROWSLEY.—An Omnibus from the Chatsworth Hotel, Edensor, meets the 8.51 & 10.3 a.m. & 2.17 p.m. Trains from Buxton & Manchester at the Rowsley Station. Post Horses & Carriages are kept at the Hotel.

The Midland Railway reached Manchester in February 1867. Some trains then ran to and from Manchester rather than Buxton, although there were generally connections to and from Buxton at Millers Dale. The footnotes to the timetable commencing May 1873 (above) now refer to omnibus connections at Hassop, Bakewell and Rowsley with Manchester trains.

Trains now called at Hassop at the following times:

Weekdays:
Down – 10.16am; 2.52pm; 4.54pm; 8.12pm
Up – 8.39am; 9.51am; 1.03pm; 5.10pm; 8.01pm

Sundays:
Down – 9.38am; 8.07pm
Up – 10.12am; 7.47pm   [G. Waite collection]

Although taken many years later, this photograph shows the proximity of the Down lie bye to the main line. A banking locomotive is seen in the lie bye, while a northbound coal train headed by an ex-L&NW Super 'D' passes on the main line.

Hassop, Hathersage, and Castleton Railway Company.

CAPITAL £60,000, IN SHARES OF £10 EACH.

DEPOSIT of £1 per Share on application, and £1 on allotment.

☞ *The liability of the Shareholders will be limited to the amount of their Shares.*

Provisional Committee.

WILLIAM CAMERON MOORE, ESQR., BAMFORD, CHAIRMAN.

ROBERT HOW ASHTON, CASTLETON.
THOMAS SOMERSET, BRADWELL.
JOSEPH R. COCKER, HATHERSAGE.
RICHARD COOKE, HATHERSAGE.
The REV. JOHN CHAMPION, EDALE.
The REV. HENRY BUCKSTONE, HOPE.

LORENZO CRISTIE, EDALE.
CHARLES GREAVES, WOODLANDS.
The REV. FRANCIS JOURDAINE, DERWENT.
JOSEPH HALL MOORE, BAMFORD.
GEORGE GIBB, CALVER.
WILLIAM BODEN, ROWSLEY.

Thomas Booth, Land.

Engineers.
MESSRS. WILKINSON AND SMITH, 31, DUKE STREET, WESTMINSTER.

Bankers.
THE SHEFFIELD AND ROTHERHAM BANK, (BAKEWELL BRANCH.)

Solicitor.
MR. JOSEPH HALL, CASTLETON, NEAR SHEFFIELD.

Secretary pro tem.
MR. HALL, CASTLETON, NEAR SHEFFIELD.

Prospectus.

At a Meeting held at Hathersage, on the 8th September, 1870, the following Resolution was passed :—

"RESOLVED—That all projects for the construction of a line of Railway through the Castleton, "Hathersage, Hope, and Derwent Valleys having failed mainly on account of the enormous expense and difficulty "of a through undertaking (as well as through the jealousies and rivalries of the great Railway Companies), this "Meeting is of opinion that the only mode of securing railway accommodation is to commence with a short single "Line to be initiated and carried through by the Landowners, Commercial Interests, and Resident Population "themselves."

This Resolution explains the grounds upon which the promoters confidently anticipate the energetic support of the Inhabitants, and others interested in the district.

The front of the prospectus for the proposed Hassop, Hathersage & Castleton Railway of 1870.

The connection to the lie bye is visible on the right of this photograph of Class 4F No.44090 of Heaton Mersey as it passes Hassop signal box with a Down train of wooden coal wagons on 29th September 1951.
[E.R. Morten]

1876	S.W. Johnson's[6] book on Water Stations on the Midland Railway records that the water tank at Hassop could hold 44,000 gallons.
August 1877	The first reference to Hassop signal box is included in the Midland Railway's Appendix No.10. This was the first appendix to show a complete list of signal boxes. The box was possibly opened around this time.

---

[6] Samuel Waite Johnson was the Midland Railway's Locomotive Superintendent. He took up his post on 2nd July 1873 and remained with the company until 31st December 1903.

14th August 1877	It was reported in *The Times* that at the Midland Railway's 67th half yearly shareholders' meeting, a *'Mr Broomhead suggested the directors should turn their attention to the making of a line from Hassop to Dore'*.
1878	The complement of staff was recorded as: Station Master 2 Clerks (one new appointment in 1874) 2 Pointsmen 2 Porters Goods Porter and Checker Machine Youth (new appointment 19th August 1872) Officer Cleaner

The Pointsmen were, in effect, signalmen. The staff records of 1870-1878 held in the PRO at Kew contain many alterations and deletions. The inclusion of two clerks appears to be somewhat suspect.

Although somewhat similar to the photograph on the cover, this view of staff on the Down platform at Hassop shows a number of differences. There is only a solitary Permanent Way employee on this occasion, while the second man on the right with the bowler hat and stick may not have been an employee of the Midland Railway. This photograph also shows the Up platform veranda and the overbridge. Note the Down side water column at the end of the platform.

18th August 1880	*The Times* for this date reports on a proposed new railway linking Dore with Hassop, together with a branch from Grindleford Bridge to Castleton (see extract from the paper on page 11). No further reports have been located. It is therefore possible that the proposal was abandoned and reconstituted in the more modest Hassop & Padley Railway scheme of 1885. By this time, of course, the Act had been passed for the Dore & Chinley Railway, which was to build the link between Dore and Grindleford.
1880	Railway Clearing House *Handbook of Stations* shows maximum crane power as 5 tons 0 cwt.
1st October 1884	The Midland Railway timetable commencing on this date includes the following about Hassop under the page relating to Coaches, Omnibuses, etc.:

'On weekdays during October only, conveyances from the Station Hotel Hassop for Chatsworth and Haddon meet the 9.50am from Manchester and the 10.30am trains from Buxton, returning in time for the 5.17pm Hassop to Buxton and Manchester. Good accommodation for Excursion Parties. Post Horses, Waggonettes etc for Baslow and neighbourhood to meet any train by previous notice A Wheeldon Proprietress.'

This shows the importance of the Station Inn at Hassop during the early years of the railway. It was also a small farm, having a limited amount of land and was rented from the Chatsworth Estate.

PROPOSED NEW RAILWAY IN DERBYSHIRE.—A scheme is on foot for opening up a most delightful part of Derbyshire which has hitherto been almost shut out from the rest of the world, and which can now only be reached by walking or by coach routes. The proposal is to make a line from the Dore and Totley Station on the Midland Railway, five miles from Sheffield, and to connect it with the Midland line at Hassop, a station on the main line from Derby to Manchester. The total distance between Dore and Hassop, according to the route proposed, is 11 miles. Shortly after leaving Dore the line will run through a magnificent stretch of moorland belonging to the Duke of Rutland, and Froggatt Edge—a high range of hills, which has hitherto been the great difficulty in opening up railway communication with that part of the country—will be cut through by a tunnel. The line will then go through a splendid valley, having Baslow on the left and Stoney Middleton and Eyam—the latter famous for its traditions of the great plague—on the right. There will be a station at Grindleford-bridge, and the line will then run on through the valley to Hassop, other stations being erected to suit the convenience of the villages along the route. It is proposed that a short line should be made somewhere in the neighbourhood of Grindleford-bridge, so as to connect the new railway with Castleton. By this means the Hope Valley, one of the most beautiful in Derbyshire, will be easily accessible. The Midland Railway promoted a line seven or eight years ago intended to serve the district now covered by the proposed scheme, but it was abandoned in consequence of the opposition of the Duke of Devonshire and the Duke of Rutland, who are the chief landowners. The present scheme meets with their approval. The line has been carefully surveyed, and meetings will shortly be held in the district for the purpose of advocating its adoption.

This Bell has been provided to enable you to call the Stationmaster or a Porter, and to intimate to the Station Staff the approach of Passenger Trains booked to stop at *Hassop* and it must be used in accordance with the following instructions :—

To Call Stationmaster	One Ring.
Up Passenger Train approaching	Two Rings.
Down Passenger Train approaching	Three „
To Call Porter	Four „

The Bell must be rung to intimate the approach of Passenger Trains as soon as the "Train entering Section" signal has been received.

Should any breach of these Regulations occur, it must be immediately reported to the Superintendent of the Line at Derby.

JOHN NOBLE,
General Manager.

Derby, *July* 1887

The report in *The Times* of 18th August 1880 which referred to a proposed railway between Dore & Totley and Hassop.

The notice to signalmen of July 1887 relating the provision of the bell for communicating with station staff. This shows the codes that had to be used. Unfortunately, the top portion of the notice is missing.

1885	Prospectus issued for the Hassop & Padley Railway. This was another abortive scheme that would have connected Hassop with the proposed Dore & Chinley Railway at Grindleford.
February 1886	An advertisement for coaches in the *High Peak News* gives the following information: *'Rowsley, Nearest Station to Chatsworth.* *The Chatsworth Hotel Omnibus meets at Rowsley the train that leaves Buxton at 10.30am… Orders for carriage to meet trains at Hassop or Rowsley ….by post or telegram, shall receive attention. – Harry Harrison, Proprietor.'* Note that in the 1864 advertisement for the Chatsworth Hotel, Hassop was shown as the station for Chatsworth.
July 1887	A bell is provided between Hassop signal box and the station to enable the signalmen to call the Station Master and porters, and to advise them when passenger trains due to call at the station are approaching.

> **HASSOP.** – During October a Waggonette from the Station Hotel, Hassop, meets the 9.35 a.m. from Manchester, and the 10.15 a.m. Trains from Buxton. Good Accommodation for Excursion Parties. Conveyances for Chatsworth, Baslow, Eyam, and neighbourhood to meet any Train by previous notice.—A. Wheeldon, Proprietress.

In the above extract from the Midland Railway's timetable for October 1891, we find that a waggonnette is now being provided by Ann Wheeldon, the proprietress of the Station Inn at Hassop.

The train service at this time was as follows:

Weekdays :
Down – 8.35am; 10.46am; 2.57pm (SO); 4.28pm; 8.18pm
Up – 8.28am; 10.33am; 10.56am; 2.16pm; 4.57pm; 6.39pm; (SO) 8.23pm

Sundays:
Down – 8.44am; 8.09pm
Up – 10.31am; 8.04pm

[G. Waite collection]

December 1892 | The Report of the Managing Committee of the Midland Railway Friendly Society for the year ending 31st December 1892 shows that two members of the Hassop station staff received sick allowance during the year. These were:

58240 Smith H.H. 10s.0d
66136 Nadin J.B. 12s.0d

1893 | Waiting Room provided on the Down Platform behind the veranda wall to add to a gents' urinal shown on the 1862 plan. Access in both cases was through the veranda wall.

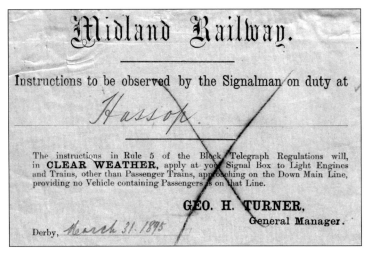

An instruction to signalmen, dated 31st March 1895, which relates to the application of Rule 5 (later Regulation 5). This allowed light engines and goods trains to be accepted from Bakewell, with the line only clear to the Down home signal. It could not be used for passenger trains. Note that the instruction applied initially to the original signal box, as it was replaced on 21st July!

21st July 1895 | Hassop Signal box renewed.

1896 | Ann & Jonathan Wheeldon shown as licensees of the Hassop Station Inn.

Left: The Hassop Station Inn taken in the mid-twentieth century after it had ceased to be used for that purpose. It was also a farm, hence the milk churns on the road side.

8th October 1896 | In October 1894, the Directors of the Midland Railway agreed to set aside a sum of money annually so that gold and silver medals could be awarded to staff in recognition of their skills in rendering First Aid.

J.B. Nadin was subsequently awarded a silver medal for rendering First Aid at Hassop. Details of the award would have been included in the annual report of the Ambulance Committee for the year ending 30th September 1897. It is recorded that a total of 24 silver medals were awarded by the Midland Railway during that period.

THE DIRECTORS of the BASLOW GAS COMPANY invite TENDERS for the CARTING of about 500 Tons of Coal from either Haassop or Grindleford for the year ending September 30th, 1898. Tenders to be in by SEPTEMBER 7th, 1897.
                                    J. R. MATTHEWMAN,
3269   Secretary.

The front and back of the silver medal awarded to J.B. Nadin for rendering First Aid at Hassop on 8th October 1896.

This photograph of the new signal box of 1895 was taken in the 1950s and shows how rural the area was. The line from the top of the Goods Shed to the left of the photograph marks the A619 road from Bakewell to Baslow and Chatsworth. The road from Hassop station joins the road from Bakewell just below the skyline on the left.   [G. Waite collection]

1900	Jonathan Wheeldon now shown as the licensee of the Hassop Station Inn.
July 1901	The timetable for July, August and September 1901 shows the following trains calling at Hassop (the service of 5 Down and 7 Up trains on weekdays, and an additional train each way on Saturdays, is an improvement over the service in operation 10 years previously):

Weekdays:
Down – 8.35am; 10.59am; 3.01pm (SX); 3.12pm (SO); 5.01pm; 7.00pm (SO); 8.55pm (a)
Up – 8.27am; 10.33am (b); 10.44am; 2.20pm; 4.57pm; 6.35pm; 8.15pm (SO); 8.30pm

Sundays:
Down – 8.44am; 8.10pm
Up – 10.34am; 8.21pm

(a) Arrives 8.47pm.
(b) Takes up passengers for London when required.

1902	Henry Moseley takes over the tenancy of the Station Inn and farm (see Appendix D).
1903	Act passed for the Grindleford, Baslow & Bakewell Railway – a further unsuccessful attempt to connect the Dore & Chinley line with the Derby to Buxton route. The Bill was read for a third time on 11th June.
1904	Railway Clearing House *Handbook of Stations* continues to show the maximum crane power as 5 tons 0 cwt. There is also another entry showing a Monsal Dale Siding located at Hassop. As there was an entry for Monsal Dale was this an error?
October 1905	A timetable amendment shows the 12.30pm MO Rowsley Sidings to Cheadle Exchange / Heaton Mersey Sidings to stop at Hassop when required to attach one wagon, and at Millers Dale to detach.
	The 12.5pm MX Rowsley Sidings to Heaton Mersey is also shown to stop at Hassop when required to attach one wagon for Millers Dale on Thursdays.
July 1906	The timetable for July, August and September 1906 shows the following trains calling at Hassop. There is another slight improvement, with 6 Down trains on a weekday:

Weekdays:
Down – 8.35am; 11.08am; 1.40pm; 2.40pm; 4.56pm; 8.46pm
Up – 9.12am; 10.31am; 11.55am; 2.11pm; 3.12pm (SO); 4.50pm; 6.13pm; 8.10pm

Sundays:
Down – 8.32am; 8.10pm
Up – 10.50am; 8.24pm

If railway enthusiasts were asked to name ten famous locomotive designs, the 'Midland Compound' would be high on most people's lists – yet the vast majority of this class were built in LMS days. For many years until the introduction of the Stanier 'Black Five' and 'Jubilee' classes in the 1930s, they were used on the expresses that ran over the 'Peak line' – quite often double-headed. In this shot, No.1021 – one of the original Midland series, which was built in April 1906 – heads an Up stopping train through Hassop in May 1934. Note the panes of glass missing from the veranda roofs. It would appear that the one on the Down side has been partially cut back.

[E.R. Morten]

c.1906	Hassop for Chatsworth reverts to Hassop in Bradshaw's timetables.
February 1907	No.3 Supplement to the Midland Railway's No.22 Appendix states:

'An electric bell has been fixed alongside the down main line about 170 yds north of the station for the purpose of signalling to drivers of engines on the down main line only. The bell is worked from the signal box and it must only be used in accordance with the instruction on page 219 of No 22 Appendix (Signalling to Drivers during shunting operations).'

1909	Water Supply:

Plan C162/09 shows a reservoir 24' x 24' x 10' deep. This was subsequently endorsed *'water supply for engines discontinued March 1910'*. The water columns were at the ends of the platforms.

April 1910	A notice issued to signalmen in relation to the use of dial signals in conjunction with the block telegraph system. This is mainly concerned with the routing of trains at Rowsley North Junction.

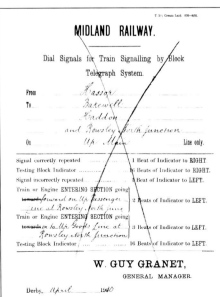

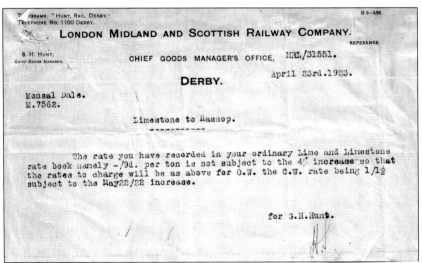

Left: The notice of April 1910 relating to the introduction of dial signals in conjunction with the block telegraph system.

July 1910	The timetable for July, August and September 1910 shows the following trains calling at Hassop. The service pattern is similar to that of 1906, but there is now an additional train each way on Sundays:

Weekdays: (Down – 6 trains : Up 7SX, 8SO)
Down – 8.34am; 11.15am; 1.40pm; 2.44pm; 5.05pm; 9.22pm
Up – 9.10am; 10.36am; 11.41am; 2.19pm; 3.53pm (SO); 4.52pm; 6.17pm; 8.14pm

Sundays:
Down – 8.29am; 11.28am; 8.13pm
Up – 11.26am; 8.06pm; 8.26pm

The number of trains calling at Hassop has now reached its peak. A gradual reduction of services appears to have commenced in October 1910.

October 1911	The timetable commencing October 1911 until further notice now shows a reduction in the number of trains calling at Hassop:

Weekdays:
Down – 8.34am; 11.09am; 1.40pm; 2.31pm (a); 5.04pm; 8.40pm (b); 9.22pm (c)
Up – 9.15am; 11.40am; 1.52pm; 2.19pm (c); 6.16pm (a) ; 8.14pm;

Sundays:
Down – 8.29am; 3.09pm (d); 8.13pm
Up – 11.26am; 8.06pm (d); 8.26pm

(a) Runs on Saturdays from 6th April and on Wednesdays from 15th May.
(b) Does not run after 30th April. Arrives Hassop at 8.25pm.
(c) Runs from 3rd May.
(d) Commencing 12th May.

17th February 1913	The *'Notice to Engine Drivers, Guards, Signalmen, Platelayers and others respecting signal alterations'* for this date states that the points in the Up Siding opposite Hassop signal box which lead into the Goods Yard will be connected to and worked from the signal box.
November 1913	Goods Traffic Accommodation:

A plan produced by the Mineral Manager's Office at Derby shows the following buildings and users of the Goods Yard:

Weigh Office and Coal Offices
Coal Yard – W. Daybell (1); T. Wright (2)
Spar Concessions Co.
Hawkins
G.G. Blackwell & Sons
Arthurton & Co.
Crane
(loading) Platform
Wagon weighbridge and office.

There was a subsequent pencil entry in respect of Roe Bros Coal Merchants (3)

Notes:
(1) previously agent to Messrs Wheatcroft.
(2) started trading in 1888.
(3) Used from the 1920s. J. MacDonald also used the Goods Yard from the 1920s to about 1952.

Amongst the traffic flows, there was:
Coal to Baslow Gas Works.
Grain and animal feed for William Gill & Sons of Calver Bridge and J. Flewitt of Ashford.
Raw cotton inwards and yarn outwards to Leicester, etc.

1914 / 1918 War	The Chatsworth Hotel at Edensor becomes a Convalescent Hospital during the Great War. Hassop is utilised as a transfer point by the Royal Army Medical Corps.
July 1915	As a consequence of the war, the average weekly mileage worked by Midland Railway passenger trains is reduced to 84.8% of that which applied in 1914. Hassop is now served by just 4 trains each way on Mondays to Fridays, with an additional service in each direction on Saturdays. Three trains continue to call on Sundays. The times of the trains are:

Weekdays:
Down – 8.36am; 11.14am; 2.37pm (SO); 5.04pm; 8.26pm
Up – 9.15am; 11.49am; 1.52pm; 6.17pm (SO) ; 8.16pm;

Sundays:
Down – 8.27am; 3.09pm; 8.11pm
Up – 11.26am; 8.06pm; 8.24pm

Members of the Royal Army Medical Corps prepare to leave Hassop station for the new Convalescent Home at Edensor during the First World War with their horses and equipment. They have probably arrived at Hassop by special train.

1st January 1917	As the war continues and more employees join the Forces, the Midland Railway is forced to make substantial reductions in the numbers of passenger trains it operates, and close both stations and lines. The timetable introduced on this date caters for only 51% of the average pre-war mileage. Hassop is not affected as much as other stations. There are still 4 weekday services on the Down line, but only 3 on the Up. The Sunday service reverts to the two trains each way pattern that operated prior to July 1910. The times of the trains are:

Weekdays:
Down – 8.28am; 11.14am; 5.04pm; 8.26pm
Up – 9.19am; 2.06pm; 9.05pm

Sundays:
Down – 8.27am; 8.11pm
Up – 11.26am; 8.24pm

c.1918	Undated Plan 9687 of the Signal Superintendents' Department shows *'Method of Underpinning Existing Timber Boxes with Concrete'* with reference to Hassop.
4th August 1920	Derwent Valley, Calver & Bakewell Railway Company's Act for connecting lines between Grindleford and Hassop. The last attempt to bridge the gap, which also failed.

Amongst the Brooke-Taylor papers at the Derbyshire County Record Office is a sketch plan of the proposed railway dated 29th October 1919, curiously headed *'Hassop Light Railway'*. Bakewell Urban District Council was originally opposed to the scheme due to a *'complete misunderstanding'*!

65

CHAPTER xcix.

An Act for incorporating the Derwent Valley Calver A.D. 1920. and Bakewell Railway Company and authorising them to construct railways in the county of Derby and for other purposes. [4th August 1920.]

WHEREAS the construction of the railways and works hereinafter described in the county of Derby would be of public and local advantage:

And whereas the persons hereinafter named with others are willing to carry the undertaking into execution on being incorporated into a company for the purpose:

And whereas it is expedient that the Company and the Midland Railway Company should be empowered to enter into and carry into effect working and other agreements as hereinafter provided and that the Midland Railway Company should be authorised and required to afford the traffic and other facilities referred to in this Act:

And whereas it is expedient that the Company should be empowered to pay interest out of capital as hereinafter provided:

And whereas plans and sections showing the lines and levels of the railways authorised by this Act and also books of reference to the plans containing the names of the owners and lessees or reputed owners and lessees and of the occupiers of the lands required or which may be taken for the purposes or under the powers of this Act were duly deposited with the clerk of the peace for the county of Derby and are hereinafter respectively referred to as the deposited plans sections and books of reference:

[*Price 3s. Net.*] A 1

Railway No. 3 (3 furlongs 1·50 chains in length) commencing in the parish of Hassop in the rural district of Bakewell by a junction with the aforesaid Railway No. 1 in a field numbered 97 on the 25-inch Ordnance map of Derbyshire (second edition 1898 sheet No. XXIII-7) at a point 16 chains or thereabouts measuring in a north-easterly direction from the centre of the junction of the four public roads adjoining the Hassop Station Inn and 3 chains or thereabouts measuring in a northerly direction from the north-western corner of the field numbered 154 on the said Ordnance map of Derbyshire (second edition 1898 sheet No. XXIII-7) and terminating in the parish of Great Longstone in the said rural district by a junction with the Midland Railway (Manchester Branch) at a point 14 chains or thereabouts measuring in a north-westerly direction along the said railway from the bridge carrying the public road over the said railway at or adjoining Hassop Station of the Midland Railway.

The front cover of the Derwent Valley, Calver & Bakewell Railway Act of 1920, together with the relevant section about the connection at Hassop. The Act was priced at 3/-. Over 40 years later, a copy was obtained from the HMSO at an amended price of 7/6d!
[G. Waite collection]

3rd October 1921	Passenger trains cease to call at Hassop on Sundays. This was shown in the *'Supplementary Working Timetable, October 1921'*. Other stations and lines were also closed on Sundays at this time. Although the inclusion of the changes implies a quick decision to effect economies, it is of note that the stops at Hassop were not included in the public timetable commencing 3rd October. No more young people from Bakewell in their 'Sunday best' would walk from that town to Hassop station and avail themselves of the 1d ride back on the train!
2nd October 1922	The last Midland Railway timetable prior to the grouping of the railways on 1st January 1923, when the Midland became a constituent of the London, Midland & Scottish Railway. There is an additional early morning Down train, making 5 in that direction, but still only 3 on the Up. The times of the trains were: Down – 7.33am; 8.34am; 11.36am; 5.13pm; 8.27pm Up – 9.02am; 5.08pm; 8.56pm It could hardly be said that this was a service to encourage people to use the station! Of the adjacent stations, Bakewell was served by 10 Down and 9 Up trains (with an additional Up train on Saturdays), while Great Longstone had 6 Down and 7 Up trains (again with an additional Up train on Saturdays).
November 1923	A local instruction to the Hassop signalmen states that if they are unable to see the Up Starting Signal from the box in fog or falling snow they must call out the fogsignalmen.
May 1926	The General Strike from 3rd to 14th May was followed on 24th May by a much reduced passenger service, which continued for several weeks, due to the shortage of coal. However, the line from Derby to Manchester was a trunk route and was not affected as much as other lines. Hassop was still served by 4 Down and 3 Up trains during this period: Down – 8.35am; 11.14am; 5.04pm; 8.26pm Up – 9.19am; 2.06pm; 9.05pm

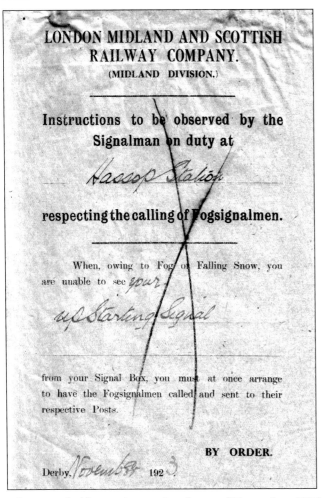

LONDON MIDLAND AND SCOTTISH RAILWAY COMPANY.
(MIDLAND DIVISION.)

Instructions to be observed by the Signalman on duty at

Hassop Station

respecting the calling of Fogsignalmen.

When, owing to Fog or Falling Snow, you are unable to see *your*

up Starting Signal

from your Signal Box, you must at once arrange to have the Fogsignalmen called and sent to their respective Posts.

BY ORDER.

Derby, *November* 192 3

L M S
LONDON MIDLAND AND SCOTTISH RAILWAY.

OPENING of HADDON HALL and GROUNDS.

On Bank-Holiday Monday, Aug. 6th, 1928,

COOK'S

Day Excursions

WILL RUN AS UNDER TO

Matlock=Bath, Matlock,
Darley Dale, Rowsley, Bakewell, Hassop, Great Longstone, and Monsal Dale,

FROM	TIMES OF STARTING. To Matlock-Bath, Matlock, and Darley Dale ONLY	To all Stations	RETURN FARES (Third Class)—to						
			Matlock-Bath	Matlock	Darley Dale	Rowsley	Bakewell	Hassop	Great Longstone	Monsal Dale
	a.m.	a.m.	s. d.	s. d.	s. d.	s. d.	s. d.	s. d.	s. d.	s. d.
LEICESTER	8.20	8.33	5 8	5 9	6 0	6 0	6 0	6 0	6 0	6 0
Syston		8.42	5 1	5 3	5 7	5 9	6 0	6 0	6 0	6 0
Sileby		8.50	4 11	5 0	5 3	5 6	5 9	6 0	6 0	6 0
Barrow-on-Soar	NON-STOP	8.55	4 7	4 9	5 0	5 3	5 8	5 9	6 0	6 0
Loughboro' ("Mid.")		9.0	4 1	4 3	4 6	4 9	5 4	5 4	5 6	5 9
Hathern		9.5	3 9	3 11	4 2	4 5	5 0	5 1	5 4	5 6
Kegworth		9.12	3 6	3 8	3 11	4 3	4 8	4 10	5 1	5 3

RETURN ARRANGEMENTS—Passengers return same day as under:—

FROM	To all Stations.	FROM	To Leicester ONLY	To all Stations
MONSAL DALE	7.10 p.m.	ROWSLEY		7.35 p.m.
GREAT LONGSTONE	7.15 p.m.	DARLEY DALE	7.10 p.m.	7.40 p.m.
HASSOP	7.20 p.m.	MATLOCK	7.15 p.m.	7.46 p.m.
BAKEWELL	7.25 p.m.	MATLOCK-BATH	7.20 p.m.	7.50 p.m.

CHILDREN under three years of age, free; three years and under twelve, half-fares

CONDITIONS OF ISSUE OF EXCURSION TICKETS AND OTHER REDUCED FARE TICKETS.

Excursion tickets and tickets issued at fares less than the ordinary fares are issued subject to the Notices and Conditions shewn in the Company's Current Time Tables.

DAY and HALF-DAY EXCURSION TICKETS.—Passengers holding day or half-day excursion tickets by special trains are not allowed to take any luggage except small handbags, or other small articles intended for the passenger's use during the day. On the return journey only, passengers may take with them, free of charge, at Owner's Risk, goods for their own use, not exceeding 60 lbs.

Passengers are requested to OBTAIN their TICKETS IN ADVANCE as this will assist the Company in the provision of accommodation.

TICKETS CAN BE PURCHASED at the STATIONS; and at the Office of THOS. COOK & SON, LTD., Gallowtree Gate, LEICESTER.

Also at LEICESTER from 3, Welford Place.

All information regarding Excursion Trains on the London Midland & Scottish Railway can be obtained on application to Divisional Passenger Commercial Superintendent, New Street Station, Birmingham, and General Superintendent (Passenger Commercial) Derby.

July, 1928.   **J. H. FOLLOWS**, Vice-President.

Sd 1075/1928   Wilkinsons (Printers) Ltd., Sheffield.   H 8,000

Above Left: The notice to signalmen of November 1923 relating to the calling out of fogsignalmen.

Above Right: Many excursions to destinations in the Peak District did not serve Hassop. This handbill for an excursion from the Leicester area on August Bank Holiday Monday 1928 is an exception. Whether such trains called after July 1931, when the hours of opening were reduced, is debatable. Certainly, the regular staff would not be still on duty at 7.20pm.

Below: An extract from a Buxton area timetable booklet showing services from 20th September 1926. An additional Up train now calls at Hassop at 1.03pm. This stop was not shown in the Winter timetables of 1922, 1923 or 1924.

[G. Waite collection]

DERBY, MATLOCK LINE AND BUXTON.

WEEKDAYS.

	a.m.	a.m.	a.m.	a.m.	a.m.	a.m.	a.m.	a.m.	a.m.	p.m.	p.m.	p.m.
DERBY ... dep.	3 55		7 5	7 48	8 7	8 40	9 45	10 8	11 15	12 25	1 8	1 15
Derby (Nottingham Rd.)			7 9		8 44			10 14		12 29		
Duffield			7 19	7 58		8 55		10 26		12 39		1 27
Belper			7 27	8 4		9 3	9 58	10 32		12 45		1 32
Ambergate			7 35	8 11	8 24	9 12	10 5	10 42		12 53		1 40
Whatstandwell			7 42					10 49		12 58		1 47
Cromford			7 50					10 56		1 4		1 53
Matlock Bath			7 55		8 36		10 17	11 1		1 8		1 59
Matlock	4 23	7 8	8 0		8 40		10 21	11 6	11 42	1 12	1 34	2 4
Darley Dale		7 14	8 8					11 13		1 17		2 10
Rowsley (for Chatsworth)		7 20	8 16					11 19				2 16
Bakewell		7 28	8 26				10 36	11 28			1 46	2 24
Hassop		7 33	8 33					11 33				
Great Longstone (for Ashford)		7 39	8 41					11 45				2 32
Monsal Dale		7 45	8 47					11 45				2 38
Miller's Dale (for Tideswell)		7 51	8 53		9 5		10 50	11 51	12 5		1 59	2 44
BUXTON ... arr.		8 3	9 10		9 25		11 15	12 22	12 22		2 15	3 14

DERBY, MATLOCK LINE AND BUXTON—continued.

WEEKDAYS.   SUNDAYS.

	p.m.	p.m.	p.m.	p.m.	p.m.	p.m.	p.m.	p.m.	p.m.	a.m.	p.m.	p.m.
DERBY ... dep.	3 40	4 68	5 42	5 48	6 55	7 10	7 18	9 2	9 5	7 5	6 20	7 0
Derby (Nottingham Rd.)	3 45		5 52					9 16		7 17		7 11
Duffield	3 57		6 2	7 5			7 30	9 22		7 22		7 16
Belper	4 2		6 7	7 12			7 39	9 29		7 32	6 37	7 26
Ambergate	4 12		6 15	7 22			7 46	9 35		7 39		7 34
Whatstandwell	4 19		6 25				7 53	9 42		7 47		7 42
Cromford	4 26		6 34				7 58	9 47		7 52	6 49	7 48
Matlock Bath	4 30		6 38				8 1	9 51		7 57	6 54	7 54
Matlock	4 35	6 12	6 43				8 8	9 57		8 3		8 0
Darley Dale	4 42	6 19	6 49				8 14	10 3		8 12	7 0	8 9
Rowsley (for Chatsworth)	4 48	6 25	6 56				8 23	10 11		8 23	7 12	8 18
Bakewell	4 56	6 32	7 3				8 28					
Hassop	5 1						8 34			8 36		8 29
Great Longstone (for Ashford)	5 7	6 40					8 40					
Monsal Dale	5 13						8 47	9 44				
Miller's Dale (for Tideswell)	5 19	5 40	6 49				8 55	9 50		8 46	7 29	8 38
BUXTON ... arr.	6 35	6 1	7 1		6 45	9 7	10 0	10 38		9 10	7 50	8 58

B—Via Chinley. Season Tickets are not available by this service unless so routed.
SO—Saturdays only.

BUXTON, MATLOCK LINE AND DERBY.

WEEKDAYS.

	a.m.	a.m.	a.m.	a.m.	a.m.	a.m.	p.m.	p.m.	p.m.	p.m.
BUXTON ... dep.	7 52	7 52	8 25	9 42	9 42	10 35	12 30	2 25	4 10	4 10
Miller's Dale (for Tideswell)	8 11	8 15	8 46	10 2	10 15	11 2	12 48	2 44	4 2	4 48
Monsal Dale			8 52				12 54			5 0
Great Longstone (for Ashford)		8 22	9 5		10 22		12 58			5 6
Hassop			9 2				1 3			
Bakewell	7 25	8 29	9 8		10 29		1 8		4 46	5 13
Rowsley (for Chatsworth)	7 33	8 36	9 17		10 36		1 15		4 47	5 22
Darley Dale	7 40	8 41	9 23		10 50		1 29		4 53	5 28
Matlock	7 47	8 46	9 30		10 57	11 22	1 35	3 2 3 44 4 57	3 44	
Matlock Bath	7 51	8 50	9 36		10 1		1 40		3 45	5 49
Cromford	7 55	8 54			11 3		1 43			5 54
Whatstandwell	8 2	9 1			11 10		1 50			6 1
Ambergate	8 9	9 8	9 52		11 18		1 56			6 7
Belper	8 18	9 14	9 58		11 26		2 3		4 3 5 16	6 16
Duffield	8 26	9 20	10 7				2 8		4 10	6 25
Derby (Nottingham Road)	8 35	9 29					2 17			
DERBY ... arr.	8 40	8 46	9 34	10 16	10 40	11 38 11 47	2 21	3 25 4 18 5 30	6 35	

BUXTON, MATLOCK LINE AND DERBY—continued.

WEEKDAYS.   SUNDAYS.

	p.m.	p.m.	p.m.	p.m.	p.m.	p.m.	p.m.	a.m.	p.m.	p.m.
BUXTON ... dep.	5 22		5 35		8 15	8 15		10 16	5 10	7 10
Miller's Dale (for Tideswell)	5 40		5 45		8 34	8 40	11 10	10 40	5 35	8 4
Monsal Dale			5 52							
Great Longstone (for Ashford)			5 55			8 50	11 17	10 47		8 13
Hassop						8 57				
Bakewell			6 2			9 10	11 24	10 54	5 46	8 23
Rowsley (for Chatsworth)			6 9			9 17	11 30	11 4	5 53	8 32
Darley Dale			6 15			9 22		11 9	5 58	8 40
Matlock		6 0	6 19	8 55	9 25			11 14	6 4	8 45
Matlock Bath		6 4	6 23	8 59	9 30			11 18	6 9	8 50
Cromford			6 26		9 33			11 21		8 55
Whatstandwell			6 30		9 40			11 28		9 2
Ambergate		6 14	6 39	9 57	9 48			11 34	6 20	9 13
Belper			6 25	6 45	9 16		10 4	11 40	6 26	9 13
Duffield			6 32	6 52			10 12	11 48	6 35	9 23
Derby (Nottingham Rd.)			6 41							
DERBY ... arr.		7 2		9 29	10 5	10 23		11 58	6 43	9 33

SO—Saturdays only.

| 1927 | The conciliation grade staff employed at Hassop were:- |

Porter Grade II

Name	DES
R. Thorpe	06.03.1917
H.W. Slaney	24.04.1924

Signalmen Class 4 (A)

Name	Porter Signlaman	To present class	Remarks
J. Brockwell	21.10.1890	31.10.1891	Fixture
D. Roberts	15.08.1892	13.01.1894	Fixture (B)
E. Townsend	09.05.1899	10.07.1912	(C)

This information is taken from an NUR Promotion List of staff on the whole of the London, Midland & Scottish Railway, which was published in December 1930. However, it is known from the entries for other locations that the information actually relates to the staffing situation in mid 1927.

(A) Classification grading made in 1928. The box was subsequently reclassified to Class 3, probably in 1951.

(B) An additional note states *'does not wish to be removed from Hassop'*.

(C) An issue of the *High Peak News* in 1945 recorded the death of **George** Townsend, late signalman Hassop, aged 72.

The Porters would have undertaken duties at both the station and in the Goods Yard.

| September 1929 | Signalmen's Instruction of 1895 relative to Rule 5 re-issued. The fog point is altered to the Down Starting Signal. |

| 22nd September 1930 | The LMS introduces a number of economies, with passenger services being withdrawn completely on some lines. Although not well patronised, Hassop is unaffected by these cuts, and continues to receive a service very similar to that which applied four years previously; |

Down – 7.33am; 8.28am; 11.33am; 5.01pm; 8.27pm
Up – 9.02am; 1.01pm; 5.04pm; 8.55pm

| December 1930 | Signalmen's Instructions of September 1929 reissued incorporating routing of trains at Rowsley North Junction. The entry reads *'Engines and freight trains requiring to go to the up passenger line at Rowsley North Junction must be signalled from Hassop to Bakewell, Haddon and Rowsley North Junction by a special train entering second signal of 2.2.2'*. The use of dial signals (see April 1910) had apparently ceased. |

LONDON MIDLAND AND SCOTTISH RAILWAY COMPANY.

INSTRUCTIONS TO BE OBSERVED BY THE SIGNALMAN ON
DUTY AT HASSOP.

1. The instructions in Block Telegraph Regulation 5 will, in clear weather, apply at your signal-box to light engines and trains, other than passenger trains, approaching on the down main line, provided no vehicle containing passengers is on that line. *Amended September 1934*

2. Engines and freight trains requiring to go on to the up passenger line at Rowsley North Junction must be signalled from Hassop to Bakewell, Haddon and Rowsley North Junction by a special Train entering section signal of 2-2-2.

3. When, owing to fog or falling snow, you are unable to see your down starting signal from your signal-box, you must at once arrange to have the fogsignalmen called and sent to their respective posts.

BY ORDER
of the
CHIEF GENERAL SUPERINTENDENT.

Derby, December, 1930.

The revised Signalmen's Instructions of December 1930.

HA

SCALE: ABT 6

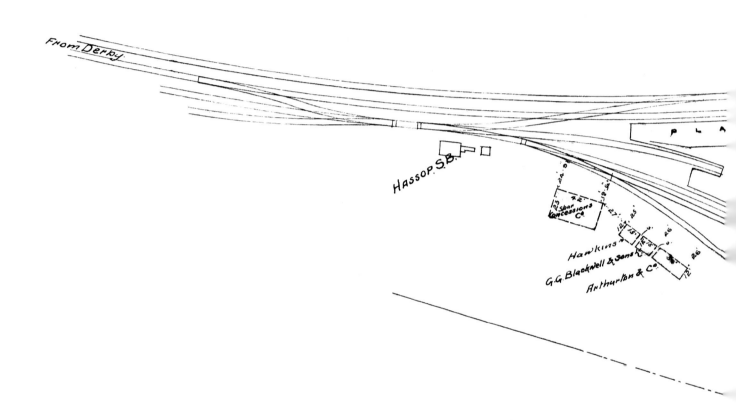

From Derby

Hassop S.B.

Concessions Co.

Hawkins
G.G. Blackwell & Sons
Arthurton & Co.

Class 3F No.43496 shunts Hassop Goods Yard
on 22nd October 1955.

SOP.

ET TO AN INCH.

Class 2P No.40404 on the 10.45am Buxton to Derby semi-fast train on 22nd October 1955. The author had a hand in the introduction of this service, which replaced a light engine working.

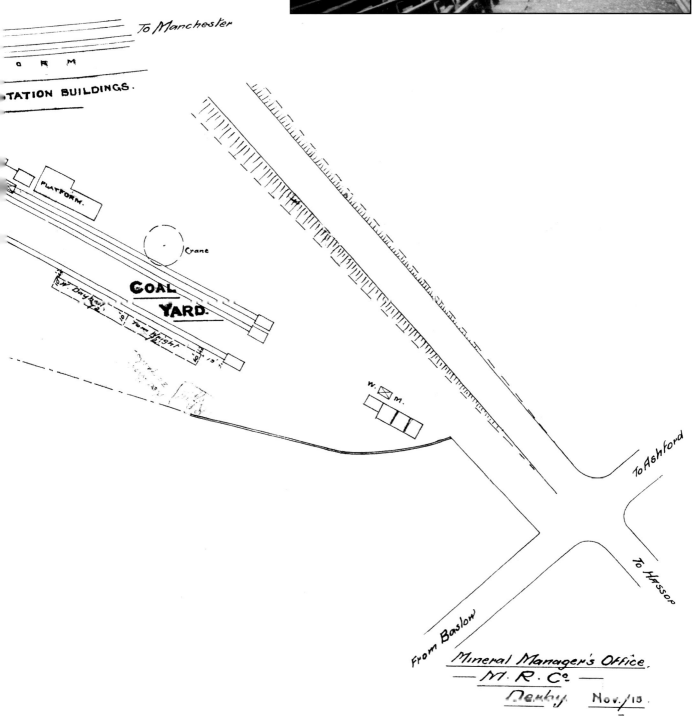

To Manchester

o R M

STATION BUILDINGS.

PLATFORM.

Crane

COAL YARD.

W. Dayku

Tom Wright

W. M.

To Ashford

To Hassop

From Baslow

Mineral Manager's Office.
M. R. Cº.
Derby   Nov./15.

January 1931	An edition of the *High Peak News* reported the retirement of Isaiah Gilbert of Little Longstone after 42 years service, 38 as Foreman Platelayer on the Hassop section. The other 4 years were spent at Peak Dale. The staff at Hassop made him a suitable presentation.
	Ganger Gilbert is credited with the lineside topiary referred to later in this chronology. It is interesting to record that his son Ernest was Ganger Longstone / Monsal Dale (later walking with a stick as a result of an accident) and grandson Reg became Ganger Hassop and later Permanent Way Sub-Inspector at Millers Dale and then at Ambergate.
July 1931	The number of passenger trains calling at Hassop station is reduced to three services in each direction, with early and late trains ceasing to stop. The trains that called were:
	Down – 8.35am; 11.33am; 5.01pm Up – 9.02am; 1.01pm; 5.04pm
	Five local trains in each direction passed through Hassop without stopping. The revised service would have enabled the work at the station to be covered by one porter.
September 1931	The following handlamps were recorded as being at Hassop: Station Master (15-B) Station (8318B and 14455B) Signalbox (B25846) Fogmen (540 and 544)
30th September 1931	'On Call' arrangements reissued by the Chief General Superintendent at Derby. The duties between Rowsley South Junction (inclusive) and Great Longstone (exclusive) were to be performed by the Station Masters at Rowsley and Bakewell. This reflects the withdrawal of the Station Master's post at Hassop (see next entry).
1st October 1931	A number of local economies are introduced by the LMS Railway.
	Hassop Station comes under the control of Ernest Clowes, the Station Master at Bakewell, while Great Longstone and Monsal Dale stations come under one Station Master.
	For some time John Townson, the Station Master at Hassop, had also been in charge of Great Longstone. The *High Peak News* for 5th September 1931 reported that he was to be transferred to Duffield in place of the Station Master there, who was retiring.
1932	The Station House was empty for a while after the departure of the Station Master, but was subsequently occupied by Tom Mullins, one of the Platelayers. One of his sons said that his father used to do reading and writing for Ganger J. Slack, who had difficulties in this direction. Tom Mullins followed the Hassop tradition of being a keen gardener and also kept plant pots in the waiting room. As cattle traffic was quite busy, including cattle from Ireland, manure was barrowed over the sleeper crossing for the station garden!
	(Frank Bebbington, a tall gangling man of some 6'2" to 6'3" was the next occupant for most of the war years and lived there to about the end of the 1940s. It is remembered that he had a large family and kept goats. He was a porter at Bakewell, and used to trudge along the line when going to or from work. Later, Richard Mansell, a District Inspector at Rowsley, occupied the house. He was another keen gardener, who constructed his own greenhouse. He was later promoted to Bletchley. A Rowsley fireman and then a relief signalman were the last railway tenants.)
Summer 1934	The LMS introduces Caravan Coaches for summer holidays; these became known as Camping Coaches in 1939. One of the coaches located in Derbyshire was at Hassop.
17th December 1934	Fogmen's overcoats: It was recorded that overcoat No.4649 was being used by T. Mullins of the Permanent Way Department and No.8859 was in Hassop signalbox for the Up Distant fog post.
July 1935	The Tariff Van booklet shows a passenger brake accompanied by a Tariff Vanman to be conveyed on the 1.15pm SX Derby to Chinley, returning on the 4.15pm ex Chinley. Only small consignments of goods traffic which could be handled without mechanical appliance were loaded in the van. These trains served Hassop in both directions although the Down train was not shown to stop in the public timetable.
1935	Census of barrows at the station:- 4-wheel (4447) – sent to Burton-on-Trent 29.09.1942 2-wheel (9606) – sent to Chinley 24.09.1941 2-wheel (2916) Sack Barrow
	The 2-wheeler was sent to Chinley was just under a year before the passenger station closed; the transfer of the 4-wheeler to Burton took place about a month after closure.

An unidentified Compound passes through Hassop with a seven coach Down express in the early 1950s. Richard Mansell's greenhouse can be seen on the near right of the photograph.

RAIL AND WALKING TOURS

FROM MATLOCK

Outward by Rail to	Returning by Rail from	Return Fare.		Approximate Walking Distance — Miles.
		1st Cl.	3rd Cl.	
		s. d.	s. d.	
Rowsley	Bakewell	1 8	1 0	4
,, ...	Hassop	1 11	1 2	4
Bakewell	,, ...	1 11	1 2	2
,, ...	Great Longstone ..	2 3	1 4	3
,, ...	Monsal Dale	2 6	1 6	1
,, ...	Millers Dale ..	3 1	1 10	8

Left A letter from the District Goods and Passenger Manger at Derby relating to the caravan coach at Hassop in 1935.

Right: Rail and Walking Tours, where passengers travelled out by rail to one station, walked to another one, and then returned from there by rail, were quite popular. This extract from an LMS booklet in the 1930s, shows the fares for a couple of 'tours' from Matlock that involved Hassop. Similar facilities were also advertised from Cromford, Matlock Bath and Darley Dale. Strangely, Hassop was not mentioned in the advertised 'tours' from Buxton.   [G. Waite collection]

> *'In the 1930s we all used Hassop Station for the Baslow Choir outing to Blackpool. Anybody could come, it didn't cost us anything. We travelled to and from Hassop in Hulley's buses, and there was a reserved carriage on the train. The train left Hassop about 9.0am, returning at 7.30pm'.*
>
> Bill Wild, former Baslow resident

1936	A circular from the Trains Office at Derby, states that 9 passenger vehicles can be run-round at Hassop. The move involves using the Up sidings.
March 1937	An additional Signalmen's Instruction issued.
	This stated that additional 'Is Line Clear' signal 1.2.2 will be received and must be forwarded whenever a train is assisted in the rear. This would only apply to the Down line.
September 1937	Signalmen's Instructions consolidated and re-issued (see document on page 25).
20th November 1938 until 22nd March 1939	Repairs carried out to Bridge No.65 – Monsal Dale Viaduct (mp 156.11 to mp 156.15) – and Bridge No.67 at Monsal Dale station (mp 156.42)
	Instructions issued respecting single line working between Hassop and Monsal Dale, which involved a temporary connection and temporary Down home signal at Hassop, which were *'only to be used as shown in the Fortnightly Notice or Supplements thereto.'*

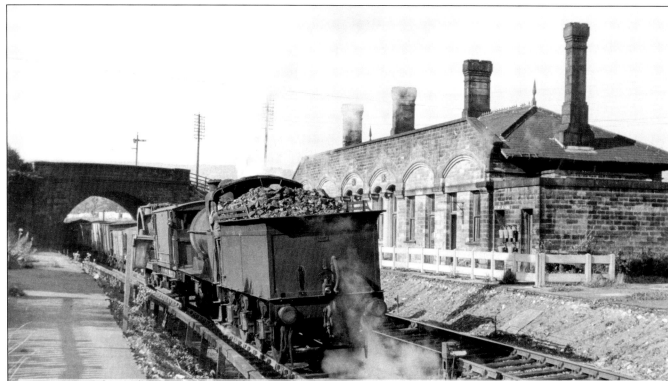

A common sight until the withdrawal of freight trains from the 'Peak line' on 3rd October 1966 – a train being banked in the rear – although in the last two years you would have found a diesel rather than a steam engine. In this photograph, taken on 29th September 1951, we have a Class 3F assisting a train through Hassop station. It will be noted that the platform edges have been cut back by this time, and concrete fencing provided on the Up platform.

[E.R. Morten]

CHEAP DAILY TICKETS.

FROM	To Derby. 3rd Class. s. d.	To Duffield. 3rd Class. s. d.	To Belper. 3rd Class. s. d.	To Ambergate. 3rd Class. s. d.	To Whatstandwell. 3rd Class. s. d.	To Cromford. 3rd Class. s. d.	To Matlock Bath. 3rd Class. s. d.	To Matlock. 3rd Class. s. d.	To Darley Dale. 3rd Class. s. d.	To Rowsley. 3rd Class. s. d.	To Bakewell. 3rd Class. s. d.	To Hassop 3rd Class. s. d.	To Gt. Longstone. 3rd Class. s. d.	To Monsal Dale. 3rd Class. s. d.	To Miller's Dale. 3rd Class. s. d.	To Buxton. 3rd Class. s. d.
DERBY	—	0 9½	1 1	1 5	1 8	2 1	2 2	2 4	2 8	2 11	3 4	3 5	3 8	3 10	4 2	4 11
DUFFIELD	0 9½	—	0 5½	0 9½	1 1	1 6	1 7	1 11	2 2	2 8	2 10	3 0	3 2	3 6	4 2	
BELPER	1 1	0 5½	—	0 5½	0 7½	1 1	1 2	1 4	1 7	1 10	2 4	2 5	2 8	2 10	3 2	3 11
AMBERGATE	1 5	0 9½	0 5½	—	0 3½	0 8½	0 9½	1 0	1 3	1 7	2 0	2 1	2 3	2 5	2 11	3 6
WHATSTANDWELL	1 8	1 1	0 7½	0 3½	—	0 5½	0 6½	0 8½	1 1	1 4	1 9	1 10	2 0	2 2	2 8	3 4
CROMFORD	2 1	1 5	1 1	0 8½	0 5½	—	0 2½	0 3½	0 7½	0 11	1 4	1 6	1 8	1 10	2 2	2 11
MATLOCK BATH	2 2	1 6	1 2	0 9½	0 6½	0 2½	—	0 2½	0 6½	0 9½	1 3	1 4	1 7	1 9	2 1	2 10
MATLOCK	2 4	1 7	1 4	1 0	0 8½	0 3½	0 2½	—	0 4½	0 7½	1 1	1 3	1 5	1 7	1 11	2 8
DARLEY DALE	2 8	1 11	1 7	1 3	1 1	0 7½	0 6½	0 4½	—	0 4½	0 9½	1 0	1 1	1 4	1 8	2 4
ROWSLEY	2 11	2 2	1 10	1 7	1 4	0 11	0 9½	0 7½	0 4½	—	0 6½	0 7½	0 9½	1 1	1 4	2 1
BAKEWELL	3 4	2 8	2 4	2 0	1 9	1 4	1 3	1 1	0 9½	0 6½	—	0 2½	0 4½	0 6½	0 11	1 7
HASSOP	3 5	2 10	2 5	2 1	1 10	1 6	1 4	1 3	1 0	0 7½	0 2½	—	0 3½	0 5½	0 9½	1 6
GREAT LONGSTONE (for Ashford)	3 8	3 0	2 8	2 3	2 0	1 8	1 7	1 5	1 1	0 9½	0 4½	0 3½	—	0 3½	0 7½	1 4
MONSAL DALE	3 10	3 2	2 10	2 5	2 2	1 10	1 9	1 7	1 4	1 1	0 6½	0 5½	0 3½	—	0 5½	1 2
MILLER'S DALE (for Tideswell)	4 2	3 6	3 2	2 11	2 8	2 2	2 1	1 11	1 8	1 4	0 11	0 9½	0 7½	0 5½	—	0 9½
BUXTON	4 11	4 2	3 11	3 6	3 4	2 11	2 10	2 8	2 4	2 1	1 7	1 6	1 4	1 2	0 9½	—

AVAILABILITY : EVERY DAY—BY ALL TRAINS.
Holders of these tickets are allowed 60 lbs. of goods free of charge purchased for their domestic use.

SEASON TICKETS.

Between DERBY and	12 Months. 1st Class. £ s. d.	12 Months. 3rd Class. £ s. d.	6 Months. 1st Class. £ s. d.	6 Months. 3rd Class. £ s. d.	3 Months. 1st Class. £ s. d.	3 Months. 3rd Class. £ s. d.	1 Month. 1st Class. £ s. d.	1 Month. 3rd Class. £ s. d.	* Weekly 1st Class. £ s. d.	* Weekly 3rd Class. £ s. d.
DUFFIELD	11 17 0	8 7 0	5 18 6	4 3 6	2 19 3	2 1 9	0 19 9	0 15 6	—	0 3 11
BELPER	15 14 0	11 5 0	7 17 0	5 12 6	3 18 6	2 16 3	1 9 0	1 0 9	—	0 5 3
AMBERGATE	18 15 0	13 16 0	9 7 6	6 18 0	4 13 9	3 9 0	1 14 6	1 5 6	—	0 6 5
WHATSTANDWELL	22 7 0	16 4 0	11 3 6	8 2 0	5 11 9	4 1 0	2 1 3	1 10 0	—	0 7 6
CROMFORD	26 15 0	19 9 0	13 7 6	9 14 6	6 13 9	4 17 3	2 9 6	1 15 9	—	0 8 11
MATLOCK BATH	28 0 0	20 2 0	14 0 0	10 1 0	7 0 0	5 0 6	2 11 6	1 17 3	—	0 9 3
MATLOCK	29 5 0	20 14 0	14 12 6	10 7 0	7 6 3	5 3 6	2 14 0	1 18 3	0 15 6	0 9 6
DARLEY DALE	31 15 0	21 19 0	15 17 6	10 19 6	7 18 9	5 9 9	2 18 6	2 0 6	—	0 10 2
ROWSLEY	35 9 0	23 17 0	17 14 6	11 18 6	8 17 3	5 19 3	3 5 6	2 4 0	—	0 11 0
BAKEWELL	38 12 0	25 15 0	19 6 0	12 17 6	9 13 0	6 8 9	3 11 0	2 7 3	—	0 11 10
HASSOP	39 11 0	26 8 0	19 15 6	13 4 0	9 17 9	6 12 0	3 12 9	2 8 9	—	—
GREAT LONGSTONE	40 10 0	27 0 0	20 5 0	13 10 0	10 2 6	6 15 0	3 16 6	2 9 9	—	—
MONSAL DALE	42 8 0	28 5 0	21 4 0	14 2 6	10 12 0	7 1 3	3 17 9	2 12 0	—	—
MILLER'S DALE	44 6 0	29 11 0	22 3 0	14 15 6	11 1 6	7 7 9	4 1 6	2 14 6	—	—
BUXTON	49 16 0	33 4 0	24 18 0	16 12 0	12 9 0	8 6 0	4 11 6	3 1 0	—	—

Tickets at corresponding rates are also issued between any two of the stations mentioned.
* To and from Derby only.

The Day Return and Season Ticket fares in operation in September 1938. In view of its poor service, it is doubtful whether Hassop had issued any season tickets for some years.

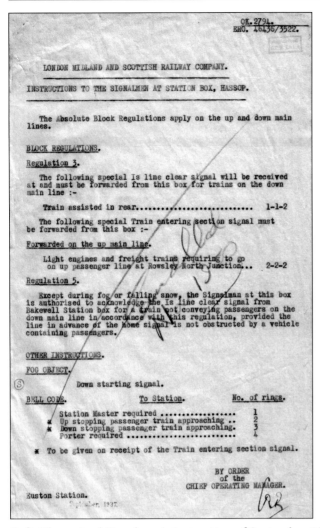

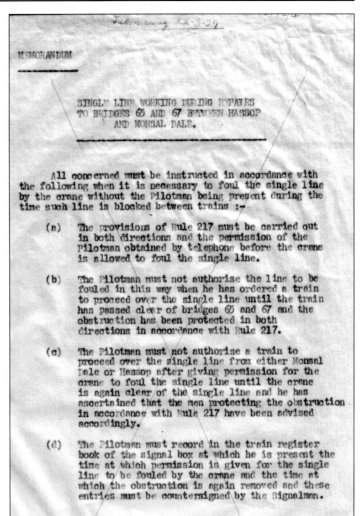

Left: The revised Signalmen's Instruction of September 1937.

Right: The instructions to signalmen in connection with single line working during the re-construction of bridges 65 and 67.

1939 to 1945	During the War, the Royal Army Service Corps was stationed at Hassop. Traffic was understood to be ammunition. This was stacked alongside the wide verges of the roads in the Monyash to Buxton areas.
16th March 1940	Staff at Hassop issued with Railway Service badges, as follows:-

Badge No.	Issued to	Grade	Note
49996	R. Thorpe	Leading Porter	
49997	F. Tubb	Porter	
49998	J.A. Mellor	Signalman	(1)
49999	L.W. Green	Signalman	(2)
50000	G. Morgan	Signalman?	(3)

(1) Later a relief signalman. Died in service.
(2) Later a signalman at Haddon and Bakewell.
(3) Returned 01.04.1940. Probably joined the Forces.

Badge No.50000 was subsequently issued to J. Smith (date not known).

Porter J. Wigley received badge No.45986 at an unknown date. He later became a shunter in Rowsley Sidings.

1940	The following handlamps were recorded as being at Hassop:

Station (8318B and 15071B)
Signal box (40977)
Fogmen (544 and 2989)

15071B was sent for repair on 9th April and was returned on 16th May.

17th August 1942	Hassop station closed for passengers – but not for parcels and miscellaneous (passenger rated) traffic. These were presumably conveyed by road motor to / from Bakewell station.

DERBY — MATLOCK — MANCHESTER

Table 3

Weekdays

	a.m.	a.m.	a.m.	p.m.	SO p.m.	p.m.	p.m.	p.m.	SO p.m.	SX p.m.	p.m.	p.m.	p.m.	p.m.		Sunday a.m.	p.m.	p.m.	p.m.	p.m.	
Derby, LMS	7 10	8 42	1010	12 5	1235	1 20	345	5 8	548	548	7 0	820	9 14	9 42	.....	7 10	12 8	5 9	530	9 7	......
Derby, NR	......	......	......	......	1239	......	......	......	......	552	......	824	......	......	......	......	......	......	.....	......	......
Duffield............	7 21	......	1021	......	1249	1 29	355	.....	6 2	6 2	......	832	......	9 52	.....	7 21	......	......	540	......	......
Belper	7 27	......	1027	......	1255	1 35	4 1	.....	6 8	6 8	......	839	......	9 58	.....	7 27	......	......	548	......	......
AMBERGATE	7 34	8 59	1034	......	1 1	1 42	4 7	.....	615	615	......	845	......	10 5	.....	7 34	......	......	555	......	......
Whatstandwell .	7 40	......	1040	......	1 6	1 48	412	.....	621	621	......	850	......	1010	.....	7 39	......	......	6 0	......	......
Cromford........	7 47	......	1047	......	1 13	1 54	419	.....	628	628	......	857	......	1018	.....	7 46	......	......	6 7	......	......
Matlock Bath	7 52	......	1052	......	1 17	1 58	428	.....	632	632	......	9 4	......	1022	.....	7 51	......	......	611	......	......
Matlock	7 58	9 11	1058	1234	1 21	2 4	433	534	638	638	726	9 8	9 41	1026	.....	7 57	1235	536	616	9 34	......
Darley Dale	8 7	......	11 7	......	1 26	2 12	440	.....	645	645	......	914	......	1032	.....	8 6	......	......	623	......	......
Rowsley	8 14	......	1115	......	......	2 17	......	.....	651	651	......	......	......	1038	.....	8 13	......	......	629	......	......
Bakewell...........	8 24	......	1126	......	......	2 27	......	.....	659	659	......	......	......	1045	.....	8 23	......	......	637	......	......
Hassop	8 30	......	1132	......	......	......	......	.....	7 3	7 3	......	......	......	......	.....	......	......	......	......	......	......
Gt. Longstone ...	8 36	......	1138	......	......	2 36	......	.....	7 9	7 9	......	......	......	......	.....	8 35	......	......	647	......	......
Monsal Dale	8 41	......	1143	......	......	2 40	......	.....	714	714	......	......	......	......	.....	......	......	......	......	......	......
Millers Dale	8 47	9 35	1149	1 2	......	2 47	......	6 0	721	721	752	......	10 7	......	.....	8 46	1 1	6 2	655	9 59	......
BUXTON ....a	9 15	1016	1211	1 22	......	3 17	......	620	......	......	811	......	1027	......	.....	9 10	1 22	622	715	1020	......
Chinley	9 20	9 54	1219	1 25	......	3 16	.....	621	750	750	314	......	1030	......	.....	9 15	1 24	625	724	1022	......
Manchester Cen	1038	1022	1 25	2 9	......	4 27	.....	652	......	......	848	......	1110	......	.....	1025	2 2	658	9 3	11 2	......

Weekdays

	a.m.	a.m.	a.m.	a.m.	a.m.	SX a.m.	SU a.m.	SO p.m.	p.m.	p.m.	p.m.	p.m.	p.m.		Sunday a.m.	a.m.	p.m.	p.m.	p.m.	p.m.	
Manchester Cen	....	....	720	7 24	8 55	1055	1055	......	2 0	242	....	550	6 45	......	7 24	8 55	2 0	242	....	550	645	....
Chinley	......	......	758	8 20	9 37	1216	1216	......	237	353	.....	629	8 19	......	8 20	9 35	237	356	......	629	811	....
BUXTON ....d	......	......	8 2	8 31	9 40	1228	1228	......	236	4 0	.....	630	8 25	......	8 25	9 40	240	4 0	......	630	820	....
Millers Dale	......	......	820	8 48	9 57	1248	1248	......	3 1	421	.....	653	8 50	......	8 48	10 1	3 1	425	......	653	840	....
Monsal Dale	......	......	......	8 54	......	1254	1254	......	.....	427	.....	......	8S56	......	......	......	......	......	......	......	......	....
Gt. Longstone ...	......	......	......	8 58	......	1258	1258	......	.....	431	.....	......	9 0	......	8 58	......	......	435	......	......	850	....
Hassop	......	......	......	9 2	......	1 2	1 2	......	.....	435	.....	......	......	......	......	......	......	......	......	......	856	....
Bakewell...........	......	732	......	9 7	......	1 7	1 7	......	.....	439	.....	......	9 7	......	9 7	......	......	444	......	......	9 3	....
Rowsley	......	739	......	9 14	......	1 15	1 15	......	.....	446	.....	......	9 15	......	9 13	......	......	451	......	......	9 8	....
Darley Dale	630	744	......	9 19	......	1 24	1 24	1 40	.....	456	.....	......	9 24	......	9 19	......	......	5 0	......	......	9 8	....
Matlock	636	749	838	9 24	1020	1 32	1 32	1 45	324	5 5	516	712	9 30	......	9 24	1024	324	5 6	......	712	914	....
Matlock Bath	640	753	......	9 28	......	1 36	......	1 50	.....	520	.....	......	9 35	......	9 28	......	......	511	......	......	918	....
Cromford.........	643	756	......	9 31	......	1 40	......	1 56	.....	523	.....	......	9 38	......	9 31	......	......	514	......	......	921	....
Whatstandwell...	649	8 2	......	9 37	......	1 46	......	2 2	.....	529	.....	......	9 46	......	9 37	......	......	520	......	......	927	....
AMBERGATE	658	811	......	9 43	......	1 53	......	2 8	.....	536	.....	......	9 52	......	9 43	......	......	527	......	......	933	....
Belper	7 5	818	......	9 49	......	2 0	......	2 14	.....	543	.....	......	9 58	......	9 49	......	......	533	......	......	939	....
Duffield............	712	825	......	9 56	......	2 8	......	2 21	.....	550	.....	......	10 4	......	9 56	......	......	541	......	......	944	....
Derby, NR	721	835	......	......	......	......	......	......	.....	......	.....	......	......	......	......	......	......	......	......	......	......	....
Derby, LMS	725	838	9 2	10 5	1045	2 17	1 55	2 30	349	531	6 0	742	1012	......	10 5	1049	349	550	......	742	953	....

SO or S—Saturday only.   SX—Saturday excepted.

The last LMS timetable to be issued showing Hassop commenced on 4th May 1942. This extract of the train service is from a later publication – the Derby ABC Guide for August of that year. Note that the restricted war time service showed only one other local train in each direction not calling at Hassop.

[G. Waite collection]

20th March 1944

A Tragedy at Monsal Dale: Signalman Ernest Griffiths aged 40, who had worked in Monsal Dale signal box for 17 years and had covered the afternoon turn on this day, was relieved by signalman A.J. Smith and commenced walking home to Great Longstone along the viaduct, intending to gain the footpath to Monsal Head. However, he was struck and killed by the 5.45pm St Pancras to Manchester express at about 10.15pm.

As he had not reached home, Driver J. Tomlinson of Rowsley in charge of a light engine, was instructed to examine the line. The *High Peak News* reported that his body was found on the viaduct at about 3.25am on the morning of the 21st and taken to Hassop station, where it was placed in the Waiting Room. It was later removed to the mortuary at Bakewell.

31st July 1945

The Smash or 'Soap Galore'

Extract from Rowsley S&T Lineman D.A. Walker's report to the Eastern Division HQ at Stoke on Trent on 1st August 1945.

Hassop – 31st July 1945
Time of incident – 3.31am
Time advice received – 3.50am at home
Time arrived – 6.30am
Time fault remedied – 5.50pm
Both main lines blocked from 3.31am to 5.50pm

A derailment of 23 wagons occurred between Hassop and Bakewell when the 9.30pm Liverpool to Nottingham Goods train, engines Nos.4177 and 4163 came derailed and occupied the Down Home Track No.1388 and Up Starter Track No.1391.

After the debris was cleared there was no apparent or material damage.

An account of the incident

The incident was actually 'train divided'. The front portion came to a stand at the Up starting signal, the driver having misunderstood the signalman's hand signal. Then the rear portion collided with the front portion, the brake van coming to a rest outside the signal box.

The smash resulted in butter, broken boxes full of soap, sugar, mailbags (Parcel post?) and ammunition being scattered about the line and adjoining field. Soap was everywhere!

Both lines were totally blocked until 5.50pm, although it took some weeks to clear up all the debris.

The train was the 9.30pm Liverpool to Nottingham, Drivers Tatam (Heaton Mersey) and Gibbons (Rowsley) on the second engine. The guard was from Heaton Mersey [but actually Cheadle Depot].

Relief Signalman A. Miles was on duty in Hassop signal box. The driver came back towards the box having not understood the train divided hand signal. It is understood the signalman, upon sighting the driver, kept shouting *'Go on! Go on!'*, but without much effect. Relief Signalman Miles was relieved by Signalman L. Harrison on the morning turn.

Crowds from Bakewell went to see what had happened, much in the manner of the old time railway disasters! The railway police arrived somewhat late in the day to safeguard property. Some accounts say even two days later!

In this time of shortages, many Bakewell folk removed soap etc to prevent it being stolen! An anecdotal tale was that a soap gatherer told another *'take plenty, there's a lot about'*, the reply being, *'I'm Detective ---------------- of Derby'* The breakdown train came from No 4 Shed at Derby. Likewise that location was inundated with soap for some months after the incident!

Drivers or firemen of engines banking Down trains used to indicate to the signalman by *'a rubbing of hands in the manner of washing'* that soap was required on the return journey. For this stop an extra allowance was required. The engine concerned would back 'inside' (off the main line).

Driver Gibbons was subsequently 'reduced' and confined to shunting within Rowsley Sidings. Because he sat as much as possible whilst on the engine, he acquired the nickname of 'Sitting Bull', most railwaymen in those days having nicknames.

1947	During the hard winter of 1947 when road conditions were difficult and *'lorries could not get anywhere'*, milk traffic again started to use Hassop station. This was probably sent to the Express Dairy Depot at Rowsley.
1948/49 to 1951	A Derby DOS area circular issued by British Railways in either 1948 or 1949, shows the platform lengths at Hassop as 100yds. This compares with Bakewell (143yds) and Rowsley (145yds), where extensions appear to have taken place.

It is believed that the platform edges were cut back (graded) and the Down side veranda wall demolished by 1950. There is evidence that the Veranda roofs had been removed as 'unsafe' some years before the station closed to passengers.

An Engineer's Plan dated January 1950 is endorsed *'Hassop Station part demolished'*. This 1950 plan showed a proposed Down Running Loop to accommodate 2 engines, 60 wagons and a brakevan. The connection from the Down Main Line was to be 585yards from the signal box. Owing to increasing freight traffic, various proposals were made to improve route capacity to the north at several locations along the line.

Also on the plan, the crossover was marked *'1949 Relaying Proposals'*. The redundant sleeper or barrow crossing between the two platforms at the south end would have been removed as part of this work.

November 1950	The bell codes from the signal box to Station are revised. There are now just two codes, both to the Station House – one for fogsignalmen and one for a lineman. It is assumed that the contact is Richard Mansell, the District Inspector at Rowsley, who then lived in the house.
27th April 1952	In the amendment to the March 1937 Appendix to the Working Time Tables, the engine whistle to be applied to freight trains and light engines on passing Hassop signal box, which were to run via the Up main line at Rowsley North Junction, was altered from 3 whistles to *'3 long 1 crow'*.

Rowsley 4F No.43929 is working hard as it passes through Hassop station with a train of mainly wooden-bodied coal wagons on 7th April 1951. The engine's tender appears to have the initials of its former owner – LMS – painted out.   [E.R. Morten]

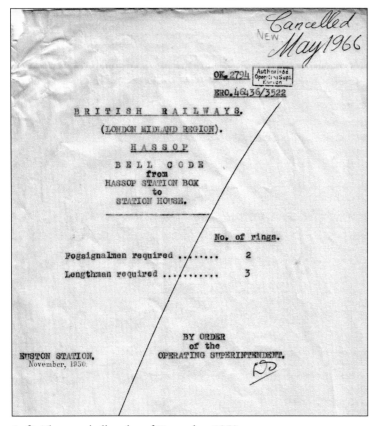

Left: The new bell codes of November 1950.

Upper Right: An atmospheric view of Compound No.41190 on the 10.24am Derby to Manchester Central on New Year's Eve 1954.

Lower Right: Class 3F No.43496 en route from Peak Forest to Rowsley after banking duties is recessed in the Hassop Goods Yard to wait the passing of an Up express on 13th October 1956.

assop – A Chronology of Railway History

The Compounds were replaced on expresses in the 1930s by new engines designed by William Stanier, first the 'Black Fives' and then in June 1938, after bridge reconstruction at Chapel-en-le-Frith, by the 5X 'Jubilees'. They remained the mainstay of the services for 20 years. In these views, we have an unidentified 'Black Five' passing through Hassop station with the 2.00pm Manchester Central to St. Pancras on 22nd April 1951, and 'Jubilee' No.45629 'Straights Settlements' on the 2.15pm St. Pancras to Manchester on 17th May 1952.   [E.R. Morten]

7th March 1953 **Derailment at Hassop**

On this Saturday evening, 0-4-4T No.58084 and vehicles M 19379 and M 24467 (Pull and Push set) worked an unadvertised train from Millers Dale to Great Longstone for students at Thornbridge Hall. The empty stock was then timed to go forward to Hassop to cross over and return to Buxton. The timings were as follows:

Buxton	dep	10.45pm	Advertised to Millers Dale
Millers Dale	arr	10.54pm	
	dep	10.55pm	
Great Longstone	arr	11.01pm	
	dep	11.03pm	ECS
Hassop	arr	11.07pm	(cross over)
	dep	11.08pm	
Buxton	arr	11.31pm	

The train was derailed on the crossover. Damage was slight, with one buffer broken, but the line was blocked until 5.0am on the Sunday. The cripple vehicles were stabled in the Dock Road. The damaged buffer was replaced on 9th March but the vehicles were not removed until 21st March. It would appear that they went to Derby C & W Works as they were noted again, repainted a 'dark red', on the 6.45am Parcels train from Derby to Buxton on 29th April with new numbers M 19379M and M 24467M.

This short-lived service, which was often subjected to cancellation as necessary, ceased to run after the June 1953 timetable.

July 1953 Up home signal renewed. Situated 12ft 6in lower and 10 yards further from the box.

These photographs, taken from the road overbridge at the station looking towards Great Longstone, show the Up home signal in both its original and new positions. In the second photograph, taken on 13th October 1956, Class 4F No.43982 of Rowsley is approaching on an Up goods train. The small signal is Hassop's Down starter. This was re-sited on the opposite side of the line 260 yards further north on 26th January 1958.

3rd August 1953 A fire on the track some 200 yards north of Hassop Station was soon extinguished by Bakewell Fire Brigade. A number of sleepers had caught fire.

September 1953 Continuing speculation about the provision of a Down loop.

15th November 1953 2.5pm Manchester to Derby, with engine No.44661, conveying four vehicles (TK BTK CK BTK), stopped specially to pick up Engineer's workmen at about 3.50pm. The train was brought nearly to a stand at the Up Home signal and then stopped by the hand signalman half way along the former Up platform. The men then clambered aboard.

2nd February 1954 Up Starter signal renewed as a colour light and combined with the Distant signal from Bakewell, 310yds from the Home signal.

February 1954 Signalling diagram 942/5 indicates:

Down catch points	580 yards from home signal
Down distant signal	575 yards from home signal
Up distant signal	1,153 yards from home signal
Up starter signal	310 yards from home signal
Up (Bakewell) distant signal	1,080 yards from home signal at Bakewell.

February 1954	Signalmen's Instructions re-issued with reference to new colour light signal.
10th August 1954	The compiler of this chronology visited the station buildings and made the following jottings:

Porters' Room	Cast iron grate broken. Wooden lockers and recess cupboards removed. Plaster falling from walls. Oil drum in cupboard recess lettered 'MR'. Three glass HASSOP signs from platform lamp cases lying on mantle piece.
Station Master's Office	Dump for waste paper, old ledgers, and circulars. Large hole in ceiling (rain soaked). At least 2 inches of water in one corner. Vegetation growing on floor. Much damp.
Waiting Room (First Class Gents)	Fair condition. No handle on door (unable to open).
Booking Office	As Leading Porter's Office was the only room in regular use. Oil lamps used in winter. Ticket rack, date presses, etc. had been removed. Midland Railway hand lamp. MR cash box repainted 'LMS Hassop'. Quantity MR books, ledgers, etc. Some boxes of cut throat razors! Generally scruffy and untidy.
Booking Hall	Dry, good condition. Locks. Used for parcels, etc. Remains of LMS sheet timetable poster. Torn / tatty posters and notices. MR oil lamp case above stone fireplace.
Ladies Room	Fairly intact. Door in order. Old Victorian waiting room chair remains. Circular walnut or elm table with decorative MR motif. Badly affected by woodworm.
	Used as joiner's shop for constructing greenhouse by District Inspector Mansell, who lived in the Station House at this time.
Waiting Room (Third Class Gents)	Fireplace semi-dismantled. Floorboards missing in places and filled with ash. Skirting boards and picture rails removed. Ceiling plaster cracked, broken laths, broken windows. Walls damp and wallpaper peeling off. Adjacent WC no roof and WC broken. Unable to shut door; exposed to all weathers.
(Rail) Weigh Office	Filled with straw. Legless chair. Platform lamp case on shelf.
Signal box	Still containing Midland Railway Telegraph instrument, which was workable. Known by some as the tick tack machine.

September 1954	Painting of Station Buildings and signal box.
	It would appear the station buildings were regarded as 'structures' being painted in silver / grey bridge paint. First paint since before the war. The signal box was painted in standard colours.
9th July 1955	Station Working & Traffic Test w/e Saturday 9th July 1955
	Hours Signalman – 10hrs £2.7s.0d, altered to £2.5s.0d. Leading Porter – 47hrs £7.12s.0d (2hrs passenger; 45hrs goods).
	Forwarded Traffic
	Mineral 21 wagons; 21 consignments; 203 tons; £368.0s.0d. Consisted of spa from Bleaklow, Longstone Edge consigned to Ickles (Rotherham), Port Talbot, etc. for the steel industry.
	(for the same period Bakewell forwarded 3 wagons; £8 receipts)

Received Traffic

Merchandise 3 wagons; 3 consignments; 21 tons (cattle cake).
Coal 7 wagons; 7 consignments; 68 tons.

(For the same period Bakewell received 9 wagons – 81 tons).

The Leading Porter at the time was Cliff Jordan, who remained at the station until closure. He earned a little more money privately by levelling the spa in the wagons after the lorries had tipped their loads.

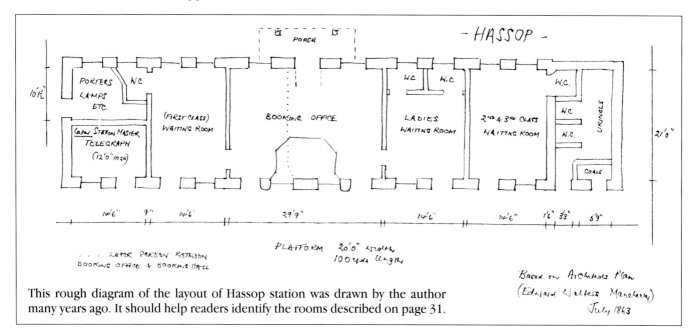

This rough diagram of the layout of Hassop station was drawn by the author many years ago. It should help readers identify the rooms described on page 31.

Class 2F No.58224 by the weighbridge during shunting operations in Hassop Goods Yard on 13th October 1956.

1956	*Handbook of Stations* indicates 3 tons 0cwt as maximum crane power (5tons 0cwt crane de-rated?)
26th January 1958	Down Starter signal renewed. 10 feet higher and positioned outside the Down Main Line 260 yards further from the box.
	The loud sounding bell applicable to setting back movements was repositioned adjacent to the new signal (but not moved on this date).
16th February 1958	Down Distant signal renewed as colour light, 65 yards further from the signal box, and 640 yards from the Home signal.
9th March 1958	Up Distant signal renewed as colour light, 290 yards further from the box, and 1,443 yards from the Home signal.
March 1958	Signalmen's Instructions re-issued, with the entry about the Fog Object deleted. This was due to the Down Starter no longer being suitable due to its re-siting on 26th January 1958.

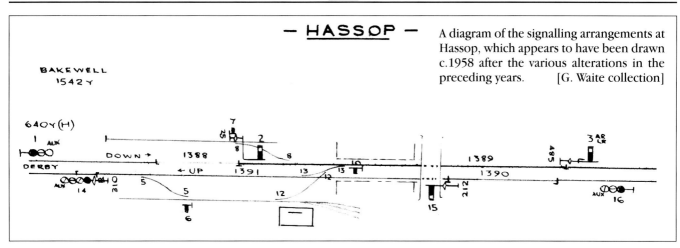

A diagram of the signalling arrangements at Hassop, which appears to have been drawn c.1958 after the various alterations in the preceding years.   [G. Waite collection]

January 1959   Signalmen's Instructions reissued to incorporate additional Bell signal relative to Buxton trains when Monsal Dale box is closed. The entry read:

'When Monsal Dale Station box is closed, the special Train entering section signal 2-2-2 must be sent for down trains going towards Buxton'.

October 1960   Supplementary Signalmen's Instructions issued:

Regulation 3

The reference to Regulation 3 is amended to read Regulation 1.

The special Is line clear signal 4-4-6 will be received and must be sent for the Midland Pullman train.

Rule 39(b)

During fog or falling snow, a train must not be allowed to draw to the down main starting signal to wait acceptance.'

Class 7P 'Royal Scots' took over some of the St Pancras to Manchester expresses at the end of the 1950s. One of the class is shown here passing Hassop signal box at the same time that two light engines are proceeding towards Rowsley.

July 1963   Signalmen's Instruction reissued to incorporate Supplementary Instructions about colour light signals. This read:

'Should the main electric power supply to the colour light up main starting signal for this box(up main distant signal for Bakewell Station box) fail, in addition to carrying out the instructions for working during such times, the signalman at this box must advise the signalman at Bakewell station box of the failure, by telephone.

The signalman at Bakewell Station box must be advised when the main electric power supply is restored.'

1963   Disused Goods Shed sold to Brian Eades for £100. Stone used for building two bungalows at Calver. Mr Eades was the Booking Clerk at Bakewell Station at the time.

1963   John I. Fearn (Agricultural) Ltd reaches agreement with British Railways Property Board to lease the station premises. These were subsequently purchased.

As a result, Leading Porter Cliff Jordan was 'evicted' from the Booking Office, and was provided with a cosy small wooden hut which was situated between the former Porters' Room and the embankment of the highway to the immediate north of the station building.

This view of Hassop signal box taken on 5th September 1963 shows the Goods Shed partly demolished in the background.
[M.A. King]

16th April 1964	Station house sold to John I. Fearn. It was subsequently derelict for many years.
April 1964	Nuttalls Scrap Depot (which had been at Hassop since September 1949) relocated to Bakewell station. All old wood and combustible materials burnt on site under 'controlled fire' arrangements. This got out of hand but nobody would take it seriously!
May 1964	Grand Opening of Agricultural Depot in the Station Buildings by farmer / radio and television personality Ted Moult.
5th October 1964	Hassop closed to Goods Traffic – total closure.
December 1964	Signalmen's Instructions reissued. Regulation 5 authority extended due to abolition of Haddon Signal box on 13th December 1964.
8th May 1966	Signal box taken out of use at 8.39am.
July 1966	Topiary:

Rail News reported that on both sides of line around Hassop, some 15 hawthorn bushes were cut to shape. These included an elephant, sheep, old woman (nearly 7ft tall!) pheasant, settee, donkey, round table, ram and fox. It is understood that these were first shaped by Ganger Isaiah Gilbert in the 1880s.

They were presently maintained by Ganger George Berresford and Lengthmen Ernie Thorpe, Ken Nuttall and Roy Tibbles.

Features concerning this topiary had appeared in newspapers and magazines over many years. They were still being maintained prior to the line's closure.

Although not particularly sharp, this photograph shows some excellent examples of the topiary that could be seen near Pineapple Bridge on the approach to Hassop station.

20th November 1966   Up line points and crossings removed and replaced by plain line.

27th November 1966   Down line points and crossings removed and replaced by plain line.

Early December 1967   Former signal box structure dismantled.

Another view from the road bridge at Hassop looking south. The signal box and Goods Shed have been removed, while the tractors in the left foreground indicate the new use of the railway premises.

June 1968	Water Supplies : It was noted that:
	Station – Lessee John I. Fearn (Agricultural) Ltd. now obtains water from Water Board. Station Farm – on Town Water but require feed to cattle trough. Troughs in field still in use. Cottages – on Town Water. Station House (sold to J.I. Fearn in 1964) will use Town supply, but gravitation until recently.
	Subsequently: Agreement (if still operative) between Midland Railway and Duke of Devonshire to be terminated from March 1970 in order that water supply to the railway premises can be blocked off.
1st July 1968	The line between Matlock and Peak Forest is closed for all purposes.
1973	Agricultural Depot extended to present size, but substantial alterations were made in 1980.
July 1986	Station House sold for £31,000. A similar amount – or more – spent on renovation!
29th April 1988	Date of conveyance for sale of Station premises, Peak Park Planning Board to J.I. Fearn for £128,565 (*Annual Report 1988-89 Peak National Park*).
1988	The Passenger Station (former J.I. Fearn Agricultural Depot) becomes the Country Bookstore.

The scene today with the trackbed now used for walking and cycling. The Up side station building, now part of the Country Bookstore, is on the left and the former Station Master's house on the right.

Appendix A

HASSOP STATION MASTERS

It will be noted that there are gaps between the dates when successive Station Masters occupied the post. The dates shown are based on documentary evidence of occupation. The changes would have taken place at unknown times between the respective dates.

S. Buxton	1862–1875	From SM Desborough; to SM Belper. His annual salary in 1862 was £80. This had increased to £120 by 1874.
J. Herbert	1875-1876	Was SM Manton; later in Goods Depot at Loughborough.
W.H. Buxton	1876-1878	Later SM Belper and SM Lincoln.
A.C. Bilham	1878-1891	Later SM Bakewell and SM Matlock Bath.
T. Peel	1891-c.1894	Born near Earby. Previously SM at Llansamlet and Six Pitt on Swansea Vale line, where a son was born.
F.J. Bent	c.1897-c.1910	
W.H. Hough	c.1912-c.1916	
U.W. Hawksley	c.1920-c.1922	
J. Townson	c.1924-1931	Transferred to Duffield

The supervision of Hassop station was transferred to the SM Bakewell from 1st October 1931.

This photograph of staff on Hassop Up platform was taken c.1900 and shows the Midland Railway uniforms of the period. At this time, the Station Master, who is standing on the left, was Frederick Bent. The tall individual next to him was the clerk, while the young fellow on the seat at the right was the junior clerk. The only person known to the author standing on the right, is James Nadin from Longstone, who served as a porter at Hassop for many years.

TRAFFIC & EXPENSES : HASSOP

Year	Season Tickets No.	Passengers Booked No.	Receipts Passengers £	Receipts Parcels etc. £	Total Coaching £	Livestock Trucks In & Out No.	Coal, Lime Coke, Limestone In & Out Tons	Carted In & Out Tons	Non-Carted In & Out Tons	Minerals In & Out Tons	Expenses £
1872		8913	875	107	986	91	4411	2220	5493	2898	490
1875		9686	866	173	1039	68	5900	2368	6351	4591	448
1880		7003	588	222	810	55	6084	1315	8699	2026	462
1885	1	6212	526	284	810	35	4694	1008	6195	3362	451
1890	1	7270	557	321	878	56	4445	1075	5898	3218	430
1895	3	4971	286	354	640	52	4974	1193	4951	3681	335
1900	1	5583	237	295	532	87	4901	1160	4691	5262	470
1905		3318	170	384	550	89	5411	902	3613	9647	465
1910		2559	180	476	656	97	6069	479	3111	9657	515
1915		2099	129	445	574	118	5577	394	3068	9721	533
1920	1	2766	386	439	825	264	5156	416	4778	10904	1572
1922	1	1760	347	523	870	147	6544	251	3171	5272	1294

Compare with Great Longstone

1872	6276
1875	9164
1880	7536
1900	14160
1922	14284

Compare with Millers Dale

1872	16451
1922	38659

Note that passenger fares were increased to 50% above pre-war levels on 1st January 1917, and to 75% above pre-war levels on 20th August 1920. There were similar rises affecting goods and mineral traffic.

[G. Waite collection]

STAFF EMPLOYED AT HASSOP

[See also entries in main chronology under 1927 (NUR Promotion List) and 1940 (Railway Service Badges)]

The station was described as a 'busy place' until the late 1930s and therefore more than one member of staff was required until the early period of the Second World War, when passenger services were withdrawn. It is probable that Bob Thorpe became Leading Porter after the Station Master's position was withdrawn in 1931.

Leading Porter

R (Bob) Thorpe	? - 1940	Transferred to Buxton as a shunter in 1940. He became a signalman at Monsal Dale in 1942, where he stayed until his retirement in 1964.
		Bob was a well-known railwayman and local personality. He and his wife also kept the Post Office and shop at Cressbrook. In recognition of being postmaster for some 40 years, he attended a Buckingham Palace garden party. He was the doyen of the Cressbrook Club and a dominoes expert.
		His father, Frank Thorpe, was a platelayer for some 44 years, retiring about 1937. His younger brother Ernie also worked for the Permanent Way Department.
Jimmy Craig	Early 1940s	Employed for a short period. Left the service.
Jack Hart	1940s – c.1950	One time Police Constable at Barrow Hill, then chauffeur to the Duke of Rutland, but required to leave ducal service upon marriage. After c.1950 employed by Bibby (cattle cake, etc.).
Cliff Jordan	c.1950 – 1964	Cliff transferred to Hassop from Rowsley where he had been a shunter. Following the withdrawal of goods facilities at Hassop, he spent his last few working days at Bakewell Passenger station attempting to issue tickets, etc., which was totally alien to him.

Cliff would not undertake lamping duties. He often spoke of an earlier life on the fish dock at Leeds Wellington. His appointment to a position at Leeds was due to his father *'transferring to the slums of Leeds'* for a few shilling promotion after previously being a Drayman at Steeton & Silsden.

Porter

Eddie Mellor	1937 / 38	Subsequently Porter / Signalman at Hurdlow, and Signalman at Haddon and Rowsley Up Sidings.
Frank Townsend	c.1938	Nicknamed 'Glider'. A one time resident of Hucklow where the Derbyshire and Lancashire Gliding Club had its headquarters. Retired as Signalman Bakewell.
F. Tubb	c.1940	
Jim Wigley	c.1940 – 1942	Post dispensed with upon withdrawal of passenger services. Later a shunter in Rowsley Sidings.

W. (Bill) Oldbury and C. Gratton were District Relief Porters who covered Hassop and other stations c.1945.

Porter Eddie Mellor (left) and Leading Porter Bob Thorpe, who was then in charge of the station, pose on Hassop Up platform c.1938. Eddie later became a signalman at Haddon and Rowsley Up Sidings, while Bob became a shunter at Buxton and a signalman at Monsal Dale. It would appear that the veranda roof has been removed. In the window is a poster advertising Holiday Contract Tickets (later Runabouts).

Signalmen

J. Mellor		[see entry below]
Stan McKay		Vice J. Mellor. Transferred to Rowsley Up Sidings
Laurence Green		Transferred to Haddon, later Bakewell.
– Griffiths	? – 1943	Transferred to Stockport Edgeley [see entry below]
Les Harrison	1943 – 1950	Vice Griffiths. Les Harrison had been a lamp lad and number taker in Rowsley Sidings since 1940. In 1943, due to the wartime shortage of staff, he was appointed Signalman Hassop at the age of 17, but as he was still a junior was not paid the full rate of pay for the job! Transferred to Rowsley North Junction in 1950. Subsequently worked in Derby and Nottingham Control Offices
Arthur Miles	1940s – 1966	Formerly a porter at Woodley (GC&M) and a Porter Signalman at Hurdlow. A Relief Signalman before transfer to Hassop. Did not suffer fools gladly. Often talked about men *'not fit to be a Signalman'*!

Herbert Bond	March 1950	Transferred to Haddon, then Matlock.
Ronald (Ronnie) Hollingsworth	1950	Transferred to Derby 'A' Box, then Spondon Station box.
Cliff Townsend	c.1950 / 1952	
Ken Robinson	1952 / 1953	Transferred to Haddon, then Bakewell.
Harold Bradwell	? – 1966	A resident of Great Longstone. Had previously been at Widnes (GC&M). Very mischievous, with tall stories that confused the uneducated!
M. Oldfield	? – 1956	Replaced by N. Hague.
Norman Hague	1956 – 1963	Replaced M. Oldfield. Possibly transferred from a relief signalman's post. Became a relief signalman on leaving Hassop and subsequently transferred to Branston Junction.
Arthur Edkins	1963 – 1966	Transferred from Rowsley South Junction on compassionate grounds (light duties)

V. Powell was a relief signalman, who covered the box in 1952.

Permanent Way Department

Lengthmen prior to the Second World War were:-

R. Gilbert   Dan Nicholson   Ernie Thorpe   Tom Mullins   J. Slack

---

Appendix D

HASSOP STATION INN AND FARM

Henry Moseley took the tenancy in 1902. He was basically a Cattle Dealer and a possible deciding factor was the proximity of railway facilities. The farm was relatively small then, land being 'taken in' in more recent times to increase the acreage. He was a respected local preacher and staunch Methodist and, therefore, did not continue with the licence for the Inn. The sale to Henry Moseley would seem to indicate that the business of the Inn had deteriorated to a very low level.

The farm continued to be worked by his son Thomas Herbert Moseley until recent times. Railway Workers – platelayers – were often used as casual labour on the farm, Ernie Thorpe being a particularly good waller.

A recent visit to Hassop Station Farm showed much remaining from its Public House days.

The main door to the Inn was from the yard but has been built over externally. Within the somewhat dark Entrance Hall is the bar with old-fashioned sash windows, permanently closed but still with counter and cash drawers. With darkish brown woodwork, the pub atmosphere is most strong here after all the years since being de-licensed. Either side of this Entrance Hall are two large rooms, the present sitting room and kitchen. Both originally had doors to the highway and were, presumably, once the Parlour and Smoke Rooms. Scratched on the glass is *'J Wheeldon 1890 W H Mossop 1888'*. Across the yard is the Coach House with *'Dance Hall'* above. There is an outside staircase and adjacent stabling.

The 'buildings' have been most altered over the years, as they were inadequate for farming purposes, being originally for stabling and for coaching. The *'Dance Hall'* or old *'Ballroom'* had a marvellous floor and once stored sacks of grain in conjunction with Flewitts Mill at Ashford. The letters *'BALLROOM'* painted on stone over the door remained for very many years after being last used for that purpose.

Hassop Station Inn c.1955.

Appendix E

ROWSLEY TRIP ENGINE

1st October 1945

No.51   Class 2 Freight Engine

	Arrive	Depart	
Rowsley Loco		7.25am	LE
Rowsley Down Sidings	–	7.50	
Bakewell	8.10am	9.03	
Hassop	9.12	11.25	
Bakewell	11.31	12.32pm	
Rowsley Sidings	12.50pm		

11th September 1961

No.58   Class 3 Freight Engine

		Arrive	Depart	
	Rowsley MPD		7.46am	LE MO
	Rowsley Down Sidings	–	8.11	MO
A	Haddon	8.25am	8.28	MO
	Bakewell	8.36	9.13	MO
	Hassop	9.20		
	Rowsley MPD		6.50	LE MX
	Rowsley Down Sidings	–	7.19	MX
A	Haddon	7.34	7.37	
	Bakewell	7.42		
		SHUNT		
	Bakewell		8.57	MX
	Hassop	9.05	–	
		SHUNT		
	Hassop		10.00	Q
	Monsal Dale	10.15	10.35	Q
	Hassop	10.45		
	Hassop		11.00	
	Bakewell	11.06	11.40	
B	Haddon	11.46	11.48	
	Rowsley Up Sidings	12.00pm		
	Rowsley Up Sidings		12.23pm	
	Darley Dale	12.33	2.20	
	Rowlsey Up Siding	2.32	–	LE
	Rowsley MPD	2.37		

A – Pick up water cans
B – Set down water cans

Class 4F No.44168 shunts Hassop Yard on New Year's Eve 1954. The Up side station building is immediately behind the engine.